"SET THEORY"

RESERVED POWER CLAUSE AND ARTICLE V

DANIEL H. MARCHI

"SET THEORY"

RESERVED POWER CLAUSE! AND ARTICLE V

ISBN (Paperback): 979-8-89672-304-2

ISBN (E-book): 979-8-89672-305-9

Printed in the United States of America.

TABLE OF CONTENTS

IV. STRUCTURE OF GOVERNMENT LAYERS

1. STATE, COUNTY, CITY, TOWN, VILLAGE SYSTEM
2. OVERLAY OF GOVERNMENT UNITS
3. INDEPENDENT DOMAINS OF AUTHORITY
4. REPUBLIC MODEL ACROSS ALL LEVELS

V. ELECTIONS AND ACCOUNTABILITY

1. ELECTION SYSTEM ACROSS GOVERNMENT LEVELS
2. EXECUTIVE POWER AND LIMITS
3. IMPEACHMENT SYSTEM (LOCAL AND FEDERAL OFFICIALS)
4. JUDICIAL ACCOUNTABILITY AND REMOVAL PROCESS
5. POPULARITY-BASED VOTING AND EVALUATION SYSTEM

VI. LEGISLATIVE EXPANSION SYSTEM

1. ADDING AMENDMENTS (STATE TO VILLAGE LEVEL)
2. ADDING BILLS (STATE TO VILLAGE LEVEL)
3. RESCINDING AMENDMENTS AND BILLS
4. CONSTITUTIONAL AMENDMENT PROCESS (ARTICLE V FRAMEWORK)

VII. EXECUTIVE POWER AND CONFLICT

1. EXECUTIVE ORDERS AND REPRESENTATION CONFLICTS
2. LIMITS OF GOVERNORS, MAYORS, AND EXECUTIVES

Introduction

This book presents a structured interpretation of constitutional governance built around a central idea: **power in a republic should flow both downward from the Constitution and upward from the people.** It explores how the United States Constitution, particularly the Tenth Amendment, can be understood as a system that divides authority between federal government, state governments, and local communities in a more balanced and measurable way.

At the foundation is the **U.S. Constitution**, which establishes the framework of national governance through its articles, and the **Bill of Rights**, which protects individual liberties. Within this structure, the **Tenth Amendment** serves as the key principle of division: it distinguishes between **delegated powers**, which belong to the federal government, and **reserved powers**, which remain with the states and the people.

This book builds on that concept to propose a broader model of governance called the **Power of Representation System**. In this model, government authority is not only defined by law, but also by **how directly it reflects the population it represents**. Representation is organized through **quasi-equal population districts**, formed using census data, ensuring that political influence is tied to population balance rather than geographic size or political boundaries alone.

The system expands across multiple levels of governance—**state, county, city, town, and village**—each functioning as its own representative structure. These levels operate under a shared principle: every layer of government holds authority only within its defined domain, while still remaining accountable to the people through structured voting systems, legislative review, and impeachment mechanisms.

A key feature of this model is the **60–40 voting structure**, designed to balance legislative decision-making with direct public participation. In addition, the system introduces mechanisms such as **add, amend, and rescind powers**, allowing laws and amendments to be created, modified, or removed through both government action and population-based approval.

The framework also includes a **computational accountability system**, where voting outcomes and public evaluations can be recorded and measured in real time. This is intended to strengthen transparency and provide continuous feedback between elected officials and the people they represent.

Beyond structure, this book also examines the relationship between **taxation, economic pressure, and governance**, particularly how federal tax systems interact with wages, corporations, and entitlement programs. It considers how these systems affect the middle class and how economic structures influence political power.

Finally, the work engages in a broader constitutional debate: the tension between **majority-rule democracy and structured republican representation**. It argues that without clear boundaries and measurable representation systems, democratic systems risk drifting toward centralized power or "mob rule," where popular influence becomes disconnected from constitutional limits.

In essence, this book is not only an analysis of constitutional law, but a **reconstruction of how representation, accountability, and power distribution could be organized across all levels of government**. It presents a unified model where governance is continuously shaped by population-based representation, structured legal authority, and active participation from the people.

Constitution

Bill of Rights

10th Amendment

Delegated Clause (Constant)
Reserved Power Clause (Variable)

This Venn diagram display illustrates the logical relations within the Constitution containing the Bill of Rights and 10th Amendment. The 10th Amendment contains the Delegated Clause which does not change or remains constant and the Reserved Power Clause which changes or is variable. Using this Venn diagram display, the Constitution becomes a living, breathing document.

Constitution

We the People of the United States, in Order to form a more perfect Union, establish Justice, ensure domestic Tranquility, provide for the common defense, promote the general Welfare, and secure the Blessings of Liberty to ourselves and our Posterity, do ordain and establish this Constitution for the United States of America.

Bill of Rights

The conventions of a number of the States having at the time of their adopting the Constitution, expressed a desire, in order to prevent misconstruction or abuse of its powers that further declaratory and restrictive clauses should be added.

Amendment I

Congress shall make no law respecting an establishment of religion, or prohibiting the free exercise thereof; or abridging the freedom of speech, or of the press; or the right of the people peaceably to assemble, and to petition the Government for a

redress of grievances.

Amendment II

A well-regulated Militia, being necessary to the security of a Free State, the right of the people to keep and bear Arms, shall not be infringed.

Amendment III

No Soldier shall, in time of peace be quartered in any house, without the consent of the Owner, nor in time of war, but in a manner to be prescribed by law.

Amendment IV

The right of the people to be secure in their persons, houses, papers, and effects, against unreasonable searches and seizures, shall not be violated, and no Warrants shall issue, but upon probable cause, supported by Oath or affirmation, and particularly describing the place to be searched, and the persons or things to be seized.

Amendment V

No person shall be held to answer for a capital, or otherwise infamous crime, unless on a presentment or indictment of a Grand Jury, except in cases arising in the land or naval forces, or in the Militia, when in actual service in time of War or public danger; nor shall any person be subject for the same offence to be twice put in jeopardy of life or limb; nor shall be compelled in any criminal case to be a witness against himself, nor be deprived of life, liberty, or property, without due process of law; nor shall private property be taken for public use, without just compensation.

Amendment VI

In all criminal prosecutions, the accused shall enjoy the right to a speedy and public trial, by an impartial jury of the State and district wherein the crime shall have been com- mitted, which district shall have been previously ascertained by law, and to be informed of the nature and cause of the accusation; to be confronted with the witnesses against him; to have compulsory process for obtaining witnesses in his favor, and to have the Assistance of Counsel for his defense.

Amendment VII

In Suits at common law, where the value in controversy shall exceed twenty dollars, the right of trial by jury shall be preserved, and no fact tried by a jury, shall be otherwise re-examined in any Court of the United States, then according to the rules of the common law.

Amendment VIII

Excessive bail shall not be required, nor excessive fines imposed, nor cruel and unusual punishments inflicted.

Amendment IX

The enumeration in the Constitution, of certain rights, shall not be construed to deny or disparage others retained by the people.

Amendment X

The powers not delegated to the United States by the Constitution, nor prohibited by it to the States, are reserved to the States respectively, or to the people.

10th Amendment

Delegated Clause

(Constant)

The Powers Delegated to The United States

Article I to VII is the delegated power of the 10th Amendment and must remain constant.

Article I

Section 1 all legislative Powers herein granted shall be vested in a Congress of the United States, which shall consist of a Senate and House of Representatives.

Section 2 Representatives and direct Taxes shall be apportioned among the several States which may be included within this Union, according to their respective Numbers, which shall be determined by adding to the whole Number of free Persons, including those bound to Service for a Term of Years, and excluding Indians not taxed, three fifths of all other Persons.

Section 3 the Senate of the United States shall be composed of two Senators from each State, chosen by the Legislature thereof, for six Years; and each Senator shall have one Vote. Immediately after they shall be assembled in Consequence of the first Election, they shall be divided as equally as may be into three Classes.

Section 7 All Bills for raising Revenue shall originate in the House of Representatives; but the Senate may propose or concur with Amendments as on other Bills.

Section 8 The Congress shall have Power To lay and collect Taxes, Duties, Imposts and Excises, to pay the Debts and provide for the common Defense and general Welfare of the United States; but all Duties, Imposts and Excises shall be uniform throughout the United States; To borrow Money on the credit of the United States; To regulate Commerce with foreign Nations, and among the several States, and with the Indian Tribes; To establish an uniform Rule of Naturalization, and uniform Laws on the subject of Bankruptcies throughout the United States; To coin Money, regulate the Value thereof, and of foreign Coin, and fix the Standard of Weights and Measures;

Article II

Section 1 The executive Power shall be vested in a President of the United States of America. He shall hold his Office during the Term of four Years, and, together with the Vice President, chosen for the same Term, be elected, as follows: Each State shall appoint, in such Manner as the Legislature thereof may direct, a Number of Electors, equal to the whole Number of Senators and Representatives to which the State may be entitled in the Congress: but no Senator or Representative, or Person holding an Office of

Trust or Profit under the United States, shall be appointed an Elector The Electors shall meet in their respective States, and vote by Ballot for two Persons, of whom one at least shall not be an Inhabitant of the same State with them- selves. And they shall make a List of all the Persons voted for, and of the Number of Votes for each; which List they shall sign and certify, and transmit sealed to the Seat of the Government of the United States, directed to the President of the Senate. The President of the Senate shall, in the Presence of the Senate and House of Representatives, open all the Certificates, and the Votes shall then be counted. The Person having the greatest Number of Votes shall be the President, if such Number be a Majority of the whole Number of Electors appointed; and if there be more than one who have such Majority, and have an equal Number of Votes, then the House of Representatives shall immediately choose by Ballot one of them for President; and if no Person have a Majority, then from the five highest on the List the said House shall in like Manner chose the President. But in choosing the President, the Votes shall be taken by States, the Representation from each State having one Vote; a quorum for this Purpose shall consist of a Member or Members from two thirds of the States, and a Majority of all the States shall be necessary to a Choice. In every Case, after the Choice of the President, the Person having the greatest Number of Votes of the Electors shall be the Vice President. But if there should remain two or more who have equal Votes, the Senate shall choose from them by Ballot the Vice President. The Congress may determine the

Time of choosing the Electors, and the Day on which they shall give their Votes; which Day shall be the same throughout the United States. No Person except a natural born Citizen, or a Citizen of the United States, at the time of the Adoption of this Constitution, shall be eligible to the Office of President; neither shall any Person be eligible to that Office who shall not have attained to the Age of thirty-five Years, and been fourteen Years a Resident within the United States. In Case of the Removal of the President from Office, or of his Death, Resignation, or Inability to discharge the Powers and Duties of the said Office, the Same shall devolve on the Vice President, and the Congress may by Law provide for the Case of Removal, Death, Resignation or Inability, both of the President and Vice President, declaring what Officer shall then act as President, and such Officer shall act accordingly, until the Disability be removed, or a President shall be elected. The President shall, at stated Times, receive for his Services, a Compensation, which shall neither be increased nor diminished during the Period for which he shall have been elected, and he shall not receive within that Period any other Emolument from the United States, or any of them. Before he enters on the Execution of his Office, he shall take the following Oath or Affirmation: "I do solemnly swear (or affirm) that I will faithfully execute the Office of President of the United States, and will to the best of my Ability, preserve, protect and defend the Constitution of the United States."

Section 2 The President shall be Commander in Chief of the Army and Navy of the United States, and of the Militia of the several States, when called into the actual Service of the United States; he may require the Opinion, in writing, of the principal Officer in each of the executive Departments, upon any Subject relating to the Duties of their respective Offices, and he shall have Power to grant Reprieves and Pardons for Offenses against the United States, except in Cases of Impeachment. He shall have Power, by and with the Advice and Consent of the Senate, to make Treaties, provided two thirds of the Senators present concur; and he shall nominate, and by and with the Advice and Consent of the Senate, shall appoint Ambassadors, other public Ministers and Consuls, Judges of the supreme Court, and all other Officers of the United States, whose Appointments are not herein otherwise provided for, and which shall be established by Law: but the Congress may by Law vest the Appointment of such inferior Officers, as they think proper, in the President alone, in the Courts of Law, or in the Heads of Departments. The President shall have Power to fill up all Vacancies that may happen during the Recess of the Senate, by granting Commissions which shall expire at the End of their next Session.

Section 3 He shall from time to time give to the Congress Information of the State of the Union, and recommend to their Consideration such Measures as he shall judge necessary and expedient; he may, on extraordinary Occasions, convene both Houses, and either of them, and in Case of Disagreement between them, with Respect to the Time of Adjournment, he may adjourn them to such Time as he shall think proper; he shall receive Ambassadors and other public Ministers; he shall take Care that the Laws be faithfully executed, and shall Commission all the Officers of the United States.

Section 4 The President, Vice President and all civil Officers of the United States, shall be removed from Office on Impeachment for, and Conviction of, Treason, Bribery, or other high Crimes and Misdemeanors.

Article III

Section 2 The judicial power shall extend to all cases, in law and equity, arising under this Constitution, the laws of the United States, and treaties made, or which shall be made, under their authority; to all cases affecting ambassadors, other public ministers and consuls; to all cases of admiralty and maritime jurisdiction; to controversies to which the United States shall be a party; to controversies between two or more states; between a state and citizens of another state; between citizens of different states; between citizens of the same state claiming lands under grants of different states; and between a state, or the citizens thereof, and foreign states, citizens, or subjects.

In all cases affecting ambassadors, other public ministers and consuls, and those in which a state shall be a party, the Supreme Court shall have original jurisdiction. In all the other cases before mentioned, the Supreme Court shall have appellate jurisdiction, both as to law and fact, with such exceptions, and under such regulations as the Congress shall make.

The trial of all crimes, except in cases of impeachment, shall be by jury; and such trial shall be held in the state where the said crimes shall have been committed; but when not committed within any state, the trial shall be at such place or places as the Congress may by law have directed.

Article IV

Section 4 The United States shall guarantee to every State in this Union a Republican Form of Government, and shall protect each of them against Invasion; and on Application of the Legislature, or of the Executive (when the Legislature cannot be convened), against domestic Violence.

Article V

The Congress, whenever two thirds of both Houses shall deem it necessary, shall propose Amendments to this Constitution, or, on the application of the Legislature of two thirds of the several States, shall call a Convention for proposing Amendments, which, in either Case, shall be valid to all Intents and Purposes, as Part of this Constitution, when ratified by the Legislature of three fourths of the several States, or by Conventions in three fourths thereof, as the one or the other Mode of Ratification may be proposed by the Congress; Provided that no Amendment which may be made prior to the Year One thousand eight hundred and eight shall in any Manner affect the first and fourth Clauses in the Ninth Section of the first Article; and that no State, without its Consent, shall be deprived of its equal Suffrage in the Senate.

Article VI

The Senators and Representatives before mentioned, and the Members of the several State Legislature, and all executive and judicial Officers, both of the United States and of the several States, shall be bound by Oath or Affirmation, to support this Constitution; but no religious Test shall ever be required as a Qualification to any Office or public Trust under the United States.

Article VII

The Ratification of the Conventions of nine States shall be sufficient for the Establishment of this Constitution between the States so ratifying the same. The Word, "the," being interlined between the seventh and eighth Lines of the first Page, The Word "Thirty" being partly written on an Erasure in the fifteenth Line of the first Page, The Words "is tried" being interlined between the thirty second and thirty third Lines of the first Page and the Word "the" being interlined between the forty third and forty fourth Lines of the second Page.

Reserved Power Clause
(Variable)

The 10th Amendment states "the powers (delegated power clause) not delegated to the United States by the Constitution, nor prohibited by it (Constitution) to the States (legislature), are reserved (reserved power clause) to the States (legislature) respectively, or to the people (quasi equal populated districts)." In other words, "the powers (delegated clause) not delegated to the United States by the Constitution, or not prohibited (not allowed) by it (Constitution) to the States (legislature), are reserved (reserved power clause) to the States (legislature) respectively, or to the people (quasi equal populated districts)." In other words, "the powers (delegated clause) not delegated to the United States by the Constitution, or not allowed by it (Constitution) to the States (legislature), are reserved (reserved power clause) to the States (legislature) respectively, or to the people (quasi equal populated districts)." In other words, "the powers (delegated clause) delegated to the United States by the Constitution, or allowed by it (Constitution) to the States (legislature), are reserved (reserved power clause) to the States (legislature) respectively, or to the people (quasi equal populated districts)."

The "reserved power clause" applies to the States legislature (quasi equal populated districts) or to the people (quasi equal populated districts). The "reserved power clause" may be applied in the following two ways:

Through the States legislature where the 60-40 voting prevails counting the number of voting legislature members Through the State people voting in "quasi equal populated districts" and the 60%-40% rule of counting the number of "quasi equal populated districts" must be in forced.

Constitution

Bill Of Rights

10th Amendment

DELEGATED ARTICLE V (CONSTANT)
ARTICLE V (INPUT)

This Venn diagram display illustrates the logical relations within the Constitution containing the Bill of Rights and 10th Amendment. The 10th Amendment contains a constant Delegated Clause Article V.

Article V is a functional input.

Using this Venn diagram display, the Constitution becomes a living breathing document.

Think Power of Representation

(State, County, City, Town, Village, In the Voting Booth)

Designated Areas (Subsets)

Designated following areas are subsets of the State area: State County City Town Village County

Designated following areas are subsets of the County area: Cities Towns Villages

Territorial Structure

The State territory is made up of contiguous State assembly "quasi equal populated districts."

The County territory is made up of contiguous County "quasi equal populated districts."

The city territory is made up of contiguous City "quasi equal populated districts."

The Town territory is made up of contiguous Town "quasi equal populated districts."

The Village territory is made up of contiguous Village "quasi equal populated districts."

Representation (Legislative / Council)

Contiguous State assembly "quasi equal populated districts" represent the State legislature.

Contiguous County "quasi equal populated districts" represent the County legislature.

Contiguous City "quasi equal populated districts" represent the city council.

Contiguous Town "quasi equal populated districts" rep- resent the Town council.

Contiguous Village "quasi equal populated districts" represent the Village council.

Essential of Republic Structure

Contiguous State assembly "quasi equal populated districts" describe an essential of a state republic.

Contiguous County "quasi equal populated districts" describe an essential of a county republic.

Contiguous City "quasi equal populated districts" describe an essential of a city republic.

Contiguous Town "quasi equal populated districts" describe an essential of a Town republic.

Contiguous Village "quasi equal populated districts" describe an essential of a Village republic.

Overlay Structure

The State assembly "quasi equal populated districts" overlay County "quasi equal populated districts."

The County "quasi equal populated districts" overlay the following:

City "quasi equal populated districts" Town "quasi equal populated districts" Village "quasi equal populated districts"

Therefore, the State assembly "quasi equal populated districts" overlay the following:

County "quasi equal populated districts" City "quasi equal populated districts" Town "quasi equal populated districts" Village "quasi equal populated districts"

Voting Booth Combinations

A person's voting booth is in one of the following combination of districts the State territory:

State "quasi equal populated districts" County "quasi equal populated districts" City "quasi equal populated districts"

Or

State "quasi equal populated districts" County "quasi equal populated districts" Town "quasi equal populated districts"

Or

State "quasi equal populated districts" County "quasi equal populated districts" Village "quasi equal populated districts"

Power of Representation (Voting)

The "power of representation" is realized casting a vote in one the following combination of districts:

State "quasi equal populated districts" County "quasi equal populated districts" City "quasi equal populated districts"

Or

State "quasi equal populated districts" County "quasi equal populated districts" Town "quasi equal populated districts"

Or

State "quasi equal populated districts" County "quasi equal populated districts" Village "quasi equal populated districts"

Candidate Representation

A person's candidates are chosen to represent ("power of representation") in one of the following combination of districts:

State "quasi equal populated districts" County "quasi equal populated districts" City "quasi equal populated districts"

Or

State "quasi equal populated districts" County "quasi equal populated districts" Town "quasi equal populated districts"

Or

State "quasi equal populated districts" County "quasi equal populated districts" Village "quasi equal populated districts"

Up Mode Power of Representation

State power is an up mode "power of representation" beginning at State "quasi equal populated districts."

County power is an up mode "power of representation" beginning at County "quasi equal populated districts."

City power is an up mode "power of representation" beginning at City "quasi equal populated districts."

Town power is an up mode "power of representation" beginning at Town "quasi equal populated districts."

Village power is an up mode "power of representation" beginning at Village "quasi equal populated districts."

House of Representative power is an up mode "power of representation" beginning at House of Representative "quasi equal populated districts."

Substitute "House" for "House of Representatives Power"

Power of Representation

"Power of representation" subsists at House of Representative power, State power, County power, City power, Town power and Village power quasi equal populated districts. Substitute House of Representative power. State power, County power, City power, Town power, and Village power with House State, County, City, Town and Village.

The 10th Amendment states, the powers (State) not delegate to the United States by the Constitution, nor prohibited by it (Constitution) to the States (legislature), are (reserved power clause) reserved to the States (legislature) respectively, or to the State people (quasi equal populated districts).

(State) is exclusive of the powers delegated to the United States.

The 10th Amendment states, the powers (County) not delegate to the United States by the Constitution, nor prohibited by it (Constitution) to the Counties (legislature), are (reserved power clause) reserved to the Counties (legislature) respectively, or to the County people (quasi equal populated districts).

(County) is exclusive of the powers delegated to the United States.

The 10th Amendment states, the powers (City) not delegate to the United States by the Constitution, nor prohibited by it (Constitution) to the Cities (council), are (reserved power clause) reserved to the Cities (council) respectively, or to the city people (quasi equal populated districts).

(City) is “exclusive of the powers delegated to the United States.

The 10th Amendment states, the powers (Town) not delegate to the United States by the Constitution, nor prohibited by it (Constitution) to the Towns (council), are (reserved power clause) reserved to the Towns (council) respectively, or to the Town people (quasi equal populated districts).

(Town) is exclusive of the powers delegated to the United States.

The 10th Amendment states, the powers (Village) not delegate to the United States by the Constitution, nor prohibited by it (Constitution) to the Villages (council), are (reserved power clause) reserved to the Villages (council) respectively, or to the Village people (quasi equal populated districts).

(Village) is exclusive of the powers delegated to the United States.

The 10th Amendment states, the powers (House) not delegate to the United States by the Constitution, nor prohibited by it (Constitution) to the House of Representatives, are (reserved power clause) reserved to the House of Representatives respectively, or to the House of Representatives people (quasi equal populated districts). (House) is exclusive of the powers delegated to the United States.

Separate Independent Domains of Power

Executive Domains of Representation

- The State governor's domain "power of representation" is the" contiguous State "quasi equal populated districts."
- The County executive's domain "power of representation" is the" contiguous County "quasi equal populated districts."
- The city mayor's domain "power of representation" is the" contiguous City "quasi equal populated districts."
- The Town mayor's domain "power of representation" is the" contiguous Town "quasi equal populated districts."
- The Village mayor's domain "power of representation" is the" contiguous Village "quasi equal populated districts."

Legislative Domains of Representation

- The State legislature's domain "power of representation" is the" contiguous State "quasi equal populated districts."
- The County legislature's domain "power of representation" is the" contiguous County "quasi equal populated districts."
- The city council's domain "power of representation" is the" contiguous City "quasi equal populated districts."
- The Town council's domain "power of representation" is the" contiguous Town "quasi equal populated districts."

- The Village council's domain "power of representation" is the" contiguous Village "quasi equal populated districts."

Structural Principles

- The State governor, County executive, City mayor, Town mayor and Village mayor are separate persons of authority.
- Likewise, state legislature, County legislature, City council, Town council and Village council are separate bodies of influence.
- Legislation creation in State legislature, County legislature, City council, Town council and Village council is independent of one another.
- The State, County, City, Town and Village are separate republics based upon contiguous "quasi equal populated districts."
- The State, County, City, Town and Village selected legislation must adhere to the Bill of Rights making the Constitution a living, breathing document including State, County, City, Town and Village.

Republics

State governments in a republic **cannot usurp power over:**

- County governments
- City governments
- Town governments
- Village governments

County governments in a republic **cannot usurp power over:**

- City governments
- Town governments
- Village governments

This is based upon the principles of **"Power of Representation"** and **"Quasi-Equal Populated Districts."**

Think Power of Representation

(State, County, City, Town, Village House)

State Power of Representation

A precursor to a state republic form of government is the construction of "quasi equal populated districts" through- out State territory using census data taken every ten years. Representative of contiguous State "quasi equal populated districts" are the elected State legislature members whom ultimately become a proportional representative body in the State legislature ruling to protect the State people "power of representation" satisfying the "reserved power clause."

The State citizens of those "quasi equal populated districts" choose the best leaders among the State people in the "quasi equal populated districts" to influence the State legislature in ruling by law protecting the State people """"power of representation.""""

The 10th Amendment states, the powers (State) not delegate to the United States by the Constitution, nor prohibited by it (Constitution) to the States (legislature), are (reserved power clause) reserved to the States (legislature) respectively, or to the State people (quasi equal populated districts).

In other words, "the powers (State) not delegated to the United States by the Constitution, or <u>not prohibited (not allowed)</u> by it (Constitution) to the States (legislature), are reserved (reserved power clause) to the States (legislature) respectively, or to the State people (quasi equal populated districts)."

In other words, "the powers (State) not delegated to the United States by the Constitution, or <u>not</u> allowed by it (Constitution) to

the States (legislature), are reserved (reserved power clause) to the States (legislature) respectively, or to the State people (quasi equal populated districts)."

In other words, "the powers (State) not delegated to the United States by the Constitution, or allowed by it (Constitution) to the States (legislature), are reserved (reserved power clause) to the States (legislature) respectively, or to the State people (quasi equal populated districts)." The "reserved power clause" applies to States legislature "quasi equal populated districts" and to the State people of "quasi equal populated districts."

The "reserved power clause" can be applied in the following two ways:

Through the State legislature where the 60-40 voting prevails counting the number of voting members.

Through the State people voting in "quasi equal populated districts" enforcing the 60%-40% rule of counting the number of winning "quasi equal populated districts"

County Power of Representation

A precursor to a county republic form of government is the construction of "quasi equal populated districts" through- out County territory using census data taken every ten years. Representative of contiguous County "quasi equal populated districts" are the elected County legislature members whom ultimately become a proportional representative body in the

County legislature ruling to protect the County people "power of representation" satisfying the "reserved power clause."

The County citizens of those "quasi equal populated districts" choose the best leaders among the County people in the "quasi equal populated districts" to influence the County legislature in ruling by law protecting the County people """"power of representation.""""

The 10th Amendment states, the powers (County) not delegate to the United States by the Constitution, nor prohibited by it (Constitution) to the Counties (legislature), are (reserved power clause) reserved to the Counties (legislature) respectively, or to the County people (quasi equal populated districts).

In other words, "the powers (County) not delegated to the United States by the Constitution, or not prohibited (not allowed) by it (Constitution) to the Counties (legislature), are reserved (reserved power clause) to the Counties (legislature) respectively, or to the County people (quasi equal populated districts)."In other words, "the powers (County) not delegated to the United States by the Constitution, or not allowed by it (Constitution) to the Counties (legislature), are reserved (reserved power clause) to the Counties (legislature) respectively, or to the County people (quasi equal populated districts)."

In other words, "the powers (County) not delegated to the United States by the Constitution, or allowed by it (Constitution) to the Counties (legislature), are reserved (reserved power clause) to the

Counties (legislature) respectively, or to the County people (quasi equal populated districts)."

The "reserved power clause" applies to County legislature "quasi equal populated districts" and to the County people of "quasi equal populated districts."

The "reserved power clause" can be applied in the following two ways:

Through the County legislature where the 60-40 voting prevails counting the number of voting members.

Through the County people voting in "quasi equal populated districts" enforcing the 60%-40% rule of counting the number of winning "quasi equal populated districts"

City Power of Representation

A precursor to a city republic form of government is the construction of "quasi equal populated districts" through- out City territory using census data taken every ten years. Representative of contiguous City "quasi equal populated districts" are the elected City council members whom ultimately become a proportional representative body in the City council ruling to protect the City people "power of representation" satisfying the "reserved power clause."

The city citizens of those "quasi equal populated districts" choose the best leaders among the city people in the "quasi equal populated districts" to influence the city council in ruling by law protecting the city people ""power of representation.""

The 10th Amendment states, the powers (City) not delegate to the United States by the Constitution, nor prohibited by it (Constitution) to the Cities (council), are (reserved power clause) reserved to the Cities (council) respectively, or to the city people (quasi equal populated districts).

In other words, "the powers (City) not delegated to the United States by the Constitution, or not prohibited (not allowed) by it (Constitution) to the Cities (council), are reserved (reserved power clause) to the Cities (council) respectively, or to the city people (quasi equal populated districts)."

In other words, "the powers (City) not delegated to the United States by the Constitution, or not allowed by it

(Constitution) to the Cities (council), are reserved (reserved power clause) to the Cities (council) respectively, or to the city people (quasi equal populated districts)."

In other words, "the powers (City) not delegated to the United States by the Constitution, or allowed by it (Constitution) to the Cities (council), are reserved (reserved power clause) to the Cities (council) respectively, or to the city people (quasi equal populated districts)." The "reserved power clause" applies to City council "quasi equal populated districts" and to the city people of "quasi equal populated districts."

The "reserved power clause" can be applied in the following two ways:

Through the City council where the 60-40 voting prevails counting the number of voting members.

Through the City people voting in "quasi equal populated districts" enforcing the 60%-40% rule of counting the number of winning "quasi equal populated districts"

Town Power of Representation

A precursor to a Town republic form of government is the construction of "quasi equal populated districts" through- out Town territory using census data taken every ten years. Representative of contiguous Town "quasi equal populated districts" are the elected Town council members whom ultimately become a proportional representative body in the Town council ruling to protect the Town people "power of representation" satisfying the "reserved power clause."

The Town citizens of those "quasi equal populated districts" choose the best leaders among the Town people in the "quasi equal populated districts" to influence the Town council in ruling by law protecting the Town people ""“power of representation.""”

The 10th Amendment states, the powers (Town) not delegate to the United States by the Constitution, nor prohibited by it (Constitution) to the Towns (council), are (reserved power clause) reserved to the Towns (council) respectively, or to the Town people (quasi equal populated districts). In other words, "the powers (Town) not delegated to the United States by the Constitution, or not prohibited (not allowed) by it (Constitution) to the Towns (council), are reserved (reserved power clause) to the Towns (council) respectively, or to the Town people (quasi equal populated districts)."

In other words, "the powers (Town) not delegated to the United States by the Constitution, or not allowed by it

(Constitution) to the Towns (council), are reserved (reserved power clause) to the Towns (council) respectively, or to the Town people (quasi equal populated districts)."

In other words, "the powers (Town) not delegated to the United States by the Constitution, or allowed by it (Constitution) to the Towns (council), are reserved (reserved power clause) to the Towns (council) respectively, or to the Town people (quasi equal populated districts)."

The "reserved power clause" applies to Town council "quasi equal populated districts" and to the Town people of "quasi equal populated districts."

The "reserved power clause" can be applied in the following two ways:

Through the Town council where the 60-40 voting prevails counting the number of voting members.

Through the Town people voting in "quasi equal populated districts" enforcing the 60%-40% rule of counting the number of winning "quasi equal populated districts"

Village Power of Representation

A precursor to a Village republic form of government is the construction of "quasi equal populated districts" through- out Village territory using census data taken every ten years. Representative of contiguous Village "quasi equal populated districts" are the elected Village council members whom ultimately become a proportional representative body in the Village council ruling to protect the Village people "power of representation" satisfying the "reserved power clause."

The Village citizens of those "quasi equal populated districts" choose the best leaders among the Village people in the "quasi equal populated districts" to influence the Village council in ruling by law protecting the Village people "“"power of representation."”"

The 10th Amendment states, the powers (Village) not delegate to the United States by the Constitution, nor prohibited by it (Constitution) to the Villages (council), are (reserved power clause) reserved to the Villages (council) respectively, or to the Village people (quasi equal populated districts).

In other words, "the powers (Village) not delegated to the United States by the Constitution, or not prohibited (not allowed) by it (Constitution) to the Villages (council), are reserved (reserved power clause) to the Villages (council) respectively, or to the Village people (quasi equal populated districts)."

In other words, "the powers (Village) not delegated to the United States by the Constitution, or not allowed by it (Constitution) to the Villages (council), are reserved (reserved power clause) to the Villages (council) respectively, or to the Village people (quasi equal populated districts)."

In other words, "the powers (Village) not delegated to the United States by the Constitution, or allowed by it (Constitution) to the Villages (council), are reserved (reserved power clause) to the Villages (council) respectively, or to the Village people (quasi equal populated districts)."

The "reserved power clause" applies to Villages council "quasi equal populated districts" and to the Village people of "quasi equal populated districts."

The "reserved power clause" can be applied in the following two ways:

Through the Village council where the 60-40 voting prevails counting the number of voting members.

Through the Village people voting in "quasi equal populated districts" enforcing the 60%-40% rule of counting the number of winning "quasi equal populated districts"

House Power of Representation

A precursor to a House republic form of government is the construction of "quasi equal populated districts" through- out House territory using census data taken every ten years. Representative of contiguous House "quasi equal populated districts" are the elected House legislature members whom ultimately become a proportional representative body in the House legislature ruling to protect the House people "power of representation" satisfying the "reserved power clause."

The House citizens of those "quasi equal populated districts" choose the best leaders among the House people in the "quasi equal populated districts" to influence the House legislature in ruling by law protecting the House people """"power of representation.""""

The 10th Amendment states, the powers (House) not delegate to the United States by the Constitution, nor prohibited by it (Constitution) to the Houses (legislature), are (reserved power clause) reserved to the Houses (legislature) respectively, or to the House people (quasi equal populated districts).

In other words, "the powers (House) not delegated to the United States by the Constitution, or <u>not prohibited (not</u> <u>allowed)</u> by it (Constitution) to the Houses (legislature), are reserved (reserved power clause) to the Houses (legislature) respectively, or to the House people (quasi equal populated districts)."

In other words, "the powers (House) not delegated to the United States by the Constitution, or <u>not</u> allowed by it (Constitution) to the Houses (legislature), are reserved (reserved power clause) to the Houses (legislature) respectively, or to the House people (quasi equal populated districts)."

In other words, "the powers (House) not delegated to the United States by the Constitution, or allowed by it (Constitution) to the Houses (legislature), are reserved (reserved power clause) to the Houses (legislature) respectively, or to the House people (quasi equal populated districts)."

The "reserved power clause" applies to Houses legislature "quasi equal populated districts" and to the House people of "quasi equal populated districts."

The "reserved power clause" can be applied in the following two ways: Through the House legislature where the 60-40 voting prevails counting the number of voting members. Through the House people voting in "quasi equal populated districts" enforcing the 60%-40% rule of counting the number of winning "quasi equal populated districts"

Reserved Power Clause

(State, County, City, Town, Village)

10th Amendment (State Power)

The powers not (State) delegated to the United States by the Constitution, nor prohibited by it to the States (legislature), are (reserved power clause) reserved to the States (legislature) respectively, or to the State people (quasi equal populated districts). (State) is exclusive of the powers delegated to the United States.

10th Amendment (County Power)

The powers not (County) delegated to the United States by the Constitution, nor prohibited by it to the Counties (legislature), are (reserved power clause) reserved to the Counties (legislature) respectively, or to the County people (quasi equal populated districts). (County) is exclusive of the powers delegated to the United States.

10th Amendment (City Power)

The powers not (City) delegated to the United States by the Constitution, nor prohibited by it to the Cities (council), are (reserved power clause) reserved to the Cities (council) respectively, or to the city people (quasi equal populated districts). (City) is exclusive of the powers delegated to the United States.

10th Amendment (Town Power)

The powers not (Town) delegated to the United States by the Constitution, nor prohibited by it to the Towns (council), are (reserved power clause) reserved to the Towns (council) respectively, or to the Town people (quasi equal populated districts). (Town) is exclusive of the powers delegated to the United States.

10th Amendment (Village Power)

The powers not (Village) delegated to the United States by the Constitution, nor prohibited by it to the Villages (council), are (reserved power clause) reserved to the Villages (council) respectively, or to the Village people (quasi equal populated districts). (Village) is exclusive of the powers delegated to the United States.

Reserved Power Clause (State Power)

The 10th Amendment states "the powers (State) not delegated to the United States by the Constitution, nor prohibited by it (Constitution) to the States (legislature), are reserved (reserved power clause) to the States (legislature) respectively, or to the State people (quasi equal populated districts)." In other words, "the powers (State) not delegated to the United States by the Constitution, or not prohibited (not allowed) by it (Constitution) to the States (legislature), are reserved (reserved power clause) to the States (legislature) respectively, or to the State people (quasi equal populated districts)." In other words, "the powers (State) not delegated to the United States by the Constitution, or not allowed by it (Constitution) to the States (legislature), are reserved (reserved power clause) to the States (legislature) respectively, or to the State people (quasi equal populated districts). In other words, "the powers (State) delegated to the United States by the Constitution, or allowed by it (Constitution) to the States (legislature), are reserved (reserved power clause) to the States (legislature) respectively, or to the State people (quasi equal populated districts)." The "reserved power clause" applies to the State (legislature) (quasi equal populated districts) or to the State people (quasi equal populated districts).

The "reserved power clause" may be applied in the following two ways:

Through the State (legislature) where the 60-40 voting prevails counting the number of voting members.

Through the State people voting in "quasi equal populated districts" and the 60%-40% rule of counting the number of winning "quasi equal populated districts" must be in forced.

Reserved Power Clause (County Power)

The 10th Amendment states "the powers (County) not delegated to the United States by the Constitution, nor prohibited by it (Constitution) to the Counties (legislature), are reserved (reserved power clause) to the Counties (legislature) respectively, or to the County people (quasi equal populated districts)." In other words, "the powers (County) not delegated to the United States by the Constitution, or not prohibited (not allowed) by it (Constitution) to the Counties (legislature), are reserved (reserved power clause) to the Counties (legislature) respectively, or to the County people (quasi equal populated districts)." In other words, "the powers (County) not delegated to the United States by the Constitution, or not allowed by it (Constitution) to the Counties (legislature), are reserved (reserved power clause) to the Counties (legislature) respectively, or to the County people (quasi equal populated districts). In other words, "the powers (County) delegated to the United States by the Constitution, or allowed by it (Constitution) to the Counties (legislature), are reserved (reserved power clause) to the Counties (legislature) respectively, or to the County people (quasi equal populated districts)." The "reserved power clause" applies to the County (legislature) (quasi equal populated districts) or to the County people (quasi equal populated districts). The "reserved power clause" may be applied in the following two ways: Through the County (legislature) where the 60-40 voting prevails counting the number of voting members. Through the County people voting in "quasi equal populated districts" and the 60%-40% rule of counting the number of winning "quasi equal populated districts" must be in forced.

Reserved Power Clause (City Power)

The 10th Amendment states "the powers (City) not delegated to the United States by the Constitution, nor prohibited by it (Constitution) to the Cities (council), are reserved (reserved power clause) to the Cities (council) respectively, or to the city people (quasi equal populated districts)." In other words, "the powers (City) not delegated to the United States by the Constitution, or not prohibited (not allowed) by it (Constitution) to the Cities (council), are reserved (reserved power clause) to the Cities (council) respectively, or to the city people (quasi equal populated districts)." In other words, "the powers (City) not delegated to the United States by the Constitution, or not allowed by it (Constitution) to the Cities (council), are reserved (reserved power clause) to the Cities (council) respectively, or to the city people (quasi equal populated districts). In other words, "the powers (City) delegated to the United States by the Constitution, or allowed by it (Constitution) to the Cities (council), are reserved (reserved power clause) to the Cities (council) respectively, or to the city people (quasi equal populated districts)." The "reserved power clause" applies to the city (council) (quasi equal populated districts) or to the city people (quasi equal populated districts).

The "reserved power clause" may be applied in the following two ways: Through the City (council) where the 60-40 voting prevails counting the number of voting members. Through the City people voting in "quasi equal populated districts" and the 60%-40% rule of counting the number of winning "quasi equal populated districts" must be in forced.

Reserved Power Clause (Town Power)

The 10th Amendment states "the powers (Town) not delegated to the United States by the Constitution, nor prohibited by it (Constitution) to the Towns (council), are reserved (reserved power clause) to the Towns (council) respectively, or to the Town people (quasi equal populated districts)." In other words, "the powers (Town) not delegated to the United States by the Constitution, or not prohibited (not allowed) by it (Constitution) to the Towns (council), are reserved (reserved power clause) to the Towns (council) respectively, or to the Town people (quasi equal populated districts)." In other words, "the powers (Town) not delegated to the United States by the Constitution, or not allowed by it (Constitution) to the Towns (council), are reserved (reserved power clause) to the Towns (council) respectively, or to the Town people (quasi equal populated districts). In other words, "the powers (Town) delegated to the United States by the Constitution, or allowed by it (Constitution) to the Towns (council), are reserved (reserved power clause) to the Towns (council) respectively, or to the Town people (quasi equal populated districts)." The "reserved power clause" applies to the Town (council) (quasi equal populated districts) or to the Town people (quasi equal populated districts). The "reserved power clause" may be applied in the following two ways: Through the Town (council) where the 60-40 voting prevails counting the number of voting members. Through the Town people voting in "quasi equal populated districts" and the 60%-40% rule of counting the number of winning "quasi equal populated districts" must be in forced.

Reserved Power Clause (Village Power)

The 10th Amendment states "the powers (Village) not delegated to the United States by the Constitution, nor prohibited by it (Constitution) to the Villages (council), are reserved (reserved power clause) to the Villages (council) respectively, or to the Village people (quasi equal populated districts)." In other words, "the powers (Village) not delegated to the United States by the Constitution, or not prohibited (not allowed) by it (Constitution) to the Villages (council), are reserved (reserved power clause) to the Villages (council) respectively, or to the Village people (quasi equal populated districts)." In other words, "the powers (Village) not delegated to the United States by the Constitution, or not allowed by it (Constitution) to the Villages (council), are reserved (reserved power clause) to the Villages (council) respectively, or to the Village people (quasi equal populated districts). In other words, "the powers (Village) delegated to the United States by the Constitution, or allowed by it (Constitution) to the Villages (council), are reserved (reserved power clause) to the Villages (council) respectively, or to the Village people (quasi equal populated districts)." The "reserved power clause" applies to the Village (council) (quasi equal populated districts) or to the Village people (quasi equal populated districts).

The "reserved power clause" may be applied in the following two ways: Through the Village (council) where the 60-40 voting prevails counting the number of voting members. Through the Village people voting in "quasi equal populated districts" and the 60%-40% rule of counting the number of winning "quasi equal populated districts" must be in forced.

"Reserved Power Clause"

Add

Amendments

(State, County, City, Town, Village House)

Constitution

Bill of Rights

10th Amendment

Delegated Clause (Constant)
Reserved Power Clause (Add State Amendment)

Add State Amendment
(A State Government Has the Power to Add an Amendment)

The 10th Amendment states "the powers (State) not delegated to the United States by the Constitution, nor prohibited by it (Constitution) to the States (legislature), are reserved (reserved power clause) to the States (legislature) respectively, or to the State people (quasi equal populated districts)."

In other words, "the powers (State) not delegated to the United States by the Constitution, or not prohibited (not allowed) by it (Constitution) to the States (legislature), are reserved (reserved power clause) to the States (legislature) respectively, or to the State people (quasi equal populated districts)."In other words, "the powers (State) not delegated to the United States by the Constitution, or not allowed by it (Constitution) to the States (legislature), are reserved (reserved power clause) to the States (legislature) respectively, or to the State people (quasi equal populated districts)."

In other words, "the powers (State) not delegated to the United States by the Constitution, or allowed by it (Constitution) to the States (legislature), are reserved (reserved power clause) to the States (legislature) respectively, or to the State people (quasi equal populated districts)."

The "reserved power clause" applies to the State legislature (quasi equal populated districts) or to the State people (quasi equal populated districts). The "reserved power clause" may be applied in the following two ways:

Add amendments through the State legislature where the 60-40 voting prevails counting the number of voting legislature members.

Add amendments through the State people voting within "quasi equal populated districts" where the 60%-40% rule prevails of counting the number of winning "quasi equal populated districts" must be in forced to add a state amendment.

The "reserved power clause" is based upon the "power of representation" within "quasi equal populate districts." Any judgment against the State amendment violates the "power of representation" within the State people "Quasi equal populated districts."

Constitution

Bill of Rights

10th Amendment

Delegated Clause (Constant)

Reserved Power Clause (Add County Amendment))

Add County Amendment

(A Country Government Has the Power to Add an Amendment)

The 10th Amendment states "the powers (County) not delegated to the United States by the Constitution, nor prohibited by it (Constitution) to the Counties (legislature), are reserved (reserved power clause) to the Counties (legislature) respectively, or to the County people (quasi equal populated districts)."

In other words, "the powers (County) not delegated to the United States by the Constitution, or not prohibited (not allowed) by it (Constitution) to the Counties (legislature), are reserved (reserved power clause) to the Counties (legislature) respectively, or to the County people (quasi equal populated districts)."

In other words, "the powers (County) not delegated to the United States by the Constitution, or not allowed by it (Constitution) to the Counties (legislature), are reserved (reserved power clause) to the Counties (legislature) respectively, or to the County people (quasi equal populated districts)."

In other words, "the powers (County) not delegated to the United States by the Constitution, or allowed by it (Constitution) to the Counties (legislature), are reserved (reserved power clause) to the Counties (legislature) respectively, or to the County people (quasi equal populated districts)."

The "reserved power clause" applies to the County legislature (quasi equal populated districts) or to the County people (quasi equal populated districts).

The "reserved power clause" may be applied in the following two ways:
Add amendments through the County legislature where the 60-40 voting prevails counting the number of voting legislature members
Add amendments through the County people voting within "quasi equal populated districts" where the 60%-40% rule prevails of counting the number of winning "quasi equal populated districts" must be in forced.
The "reserved power clause" is based upon the "power of representation" within the County "quasi equal populate districts."
Any judgment against the County amendment violates the "power of representation" within the County people "quasi equal populated districts."

Constitution

Bill of Rights

10th Amendment

Delegated Clause (Constant)

Reserved Power Clause (Add City Amendment)

Add City Amendment

(A City Government Has the Power to Add an Amendment)

The 10th Amendment states "the powers (City) not delegated to the United States by the Constitution, nor prohibited by it (Constitution) to the Cities (council), are reserved (reserved power clause) to the Cities (council) respectively, or to the city people (quasi equal populated districts)."

In other words, "the powers (City) not delegated to the United States by the Constitution, or not prohibited (not allowed) by it (Constitution) to the Cities (council), are reserved (reserved power clause) to the Cities (council) respectively, or to the city people (quasi equal populated districts)."

In other words, "the powers (City) not delegated to the United States by the Constitution, or not allowed by it (Constitution) to the Cities (council), are reserved (reserved power clause) to the

Cities (council) respectively, or to the city people (quasi equal populated districts)."

In other words, "the powers (City) not delegated to the United States by the Constitution, or allowed by it (Constitution) to the Cities (council), are reserved (reserved power clause) to the Cities (council) respectively, or to the city people (quasi equal populated districts)."

The "reserved power clause" applies to the city council (quasi equal populated districts) or to the city people (quasi equal populated districts).

The "reserved power clause" may be applied in the following two ways: Add amendments through the city council where the 60-40 voting prevails counting the number of voting legislature members.

Add amendments through the City people voting within "quasi equal populated districts" where the 60%-40% rule prevails of counting the number of winning "quasi equal populated districts" must be in forced.

The "reserved power clause" is based upon the "power of representation" within the City "quasi equal populate districts." Any judgment against the city amendment violates the "power of representation" within the city people "quasi equal populated districts."

Constitution

Bill of Rights

10th Amendment

Delegated Clause (Constant)
Reserved Power Clause (Add Town Amendment)

Add Town Amendment
(A Town Government Has the Power to Add an Amendment)

The 10th Amendment states "the powers (Town) not delegated to the United States by the Constitution, nor prohibited by it (Constitution) to the Towns (council), are reserved (reserved power clause) to the Towns (council) respectively, or to the Town people (quasi equal populated districts)."

In other words, "the powers (Town) not delegated to the United States by the Constitution, or not prohibited (not allowed) by it (Constitution) to the Towns (council), are reserved (reserved power clause) to the Towns (council) respectively, or to the Town people (quasi equal populated districts)." In other words, "the powers (Town) not delegated to the United States by the Constitution, or not allowed by it (Constitution) to the Towns (council), are reserved (reserved power clause) to the Towns (council) respectively, or to the Town people (quasi equal populated districts)."

In other words, "the powers (Town) not delegated to the United States by the Constitution, or allowed by it (Constitution) to the Towns (council), are reserved (reserved power clause) to the Towns (council) respectively, or to the Town people (quasi equal populated districts)."

The "reserved power clause" applies to the Town council (quasi equal populated districts) or to the Town people (quasi equal populated districts). The "reserved power clause" may be applied in the following two ways:

Add amendments through the Town council where the 60-40 voting prevails counting the number of voting legislature members.

Add amendments through the Town people voting within "quasi equal populated districts" where the 60%-40% rule prevails of counting the number of winning "quasi equal populated districts" must be in forced.

The "reserved power clause" is based upon the "power of representation" within the Town "quasi equal populate districts." Any judgment against the Town amendment violates the "power of representation" within the Town people "quasi equal populated districts."

Constitution

Bill of Rights

10th Amendment

Delegated Clause (Constant)
Reserved Power Clause (Add Village Amendment))

Add Village Amendment
(A Village Government Has the Power to Add an Amendment)

The 10th Amendment states "the powers (Village) not delegated to the United States by the Constitution, nor prohibited by it (Constitution) to the Villages (council), are reserved (reserved power clause) to the Villages (council) respectively, or to the Village people (quasi equal populated districts)."

In other words, "the powers (Village) not delegated to the United States by the Constitution, or not prohibited (not allowed) by it (Constitution) to the Villages (council), are reserved (reserved power clause) to the Villages (council) respectively, or to the Village people (quasi equal populated districts)."

In other words, "the powers (Village) not delegated to the United States by the Constitution, or not allowed by it (Constitution) to the Villages (council), are reserved (reserved power clause) to the

Villages (council) respectively, or to the Village people (quasi equal populated districts)."

In other words, "the powers (Village) not delegated to the United States by the Constitution, or allowed by it (Constitution) to the Villages (council), are reserved (reserved power clause) to the Villages (council) respectively, or to the Village people (quasi equal populated districts)."

The "reserved power clause" applies to the Village council (quasi equal populated districts) or to the Village people (quasi equal populated districts).

The "reserved power clause" may be applied in the following two ways: Add amendments through the Village council where the 60-40 voting prevails counting the number of voting legislature members.

Add amendments through the Village people voting within "quasi equal populated districts" where the 60%-40% rule prevails of counting the number of winning "quasi equal populated districts" must be in forced.

The "reserved power clause" is based upon the "power of representation" within the Village "quasi equal populate districts." Any judgment against the Village amendment violates the "power of representation" within the Village people "quasi equal populated districts."

Constitution

Bill of Rights

10th Amendment

Delegated Clause (Constant)

Reserved Power Clause (Add House Amendment))

Add House Amendment

(A House Government Has the Power to Add an Amendment)

The 10th Amendment states "the powers (House) not delegated to the United States by the Constitution, nor prohibited by it (Constitution) to the Houses (legislature), are reserved (reserved power clause) to the Houses (legislature) respectively, or to the House people (quasi equal populated districts)."

In other words, "the powers (House) not delegated to the United States by the Constitution, or not prohibited (not allowed) by it (Constitution) to the Houses (legislature), are reserved (reserved power clause) to the Houses (legislature) respectively, or to the House people (quasi equal populated districts)."

In other words, "the powers (House) not delegated to the United States by the Constitution, or not allowed by it (Constitution) to the Houses (legislature), are reserved (reserved power clause) to

the Houses (legislature) respectively, or to the House people (quasi equal populated districts)."

In other words, "the powers (House) not delegated to the United States by the Constitution, or allowed by it (Constitution) to the Houses (legislature), are reserved (reserved power clause) to the Houses (legislature) respectively, or to the House people (quasi equal populated districts)."

The "reserved power clause" applies to the House legislature (quasi equal populated districts) or to the House people (quasi equal populated districts).

The "reserved power clause" may be applied in the following two ways: Add amendments through the House legislature where the 60-40 voting prevails counting the number of voting legislature members.
Add amendments through the House people voting within "quasi equal populated districts" where the 60%-40% rule prevails of counting the number of winning "quasi equal populated districts" must be in forced.
The "reserved power clause" is based upon the "power of representation" within the House "quasi equal populate districts." Any judgment against the House amendment violates the "power of representation" within the House people "quasi equal populated districts."

“Reserved Power Clause”

Add Bills

(State, County, City, Town, Village House)

Constitution

Bill of Rights

10th Amendment

Delegated Clause (Constant)

Reserved Power Clause (Add State Bill)

Add State Amendment

(A State Government Has the Power to Add a bill)

The 10th Amendment states "the powers (State) not delegated to the United States by the Constitution, nor prohibited by it (Constitution) to the States (legislature), are reserved (reserved power clause) to the States (legislature) respectively, or to the State people (quasi equal populated districts)."

In other words, "the powers (State) not delegated to the United States by the Constitution, or not prohibited (not allowed) by it (Constitution) to the States (legislature), are reserved (reserved power clause) to the States (legislature) respectively, or to the State people (quasi equal populated districts)."

In other words, "the powers (State) not delegated to the United States by the Constitution, or not allowed by it (Constitution) to the States (legislature), are reserved (reserved power clause) to the States (legislature) respectively, or to the State people (quasi equal populated districts)." In other words, "the powers (State) not delegated to the United States by the Constitution, or allowed by it (Constitution) to the States (legislature), are reserved (reserved power clause) to the States (legislature) respectively, or to the State people (quasi equal populated districts)." The "reserved power clause" applies to the State legislature (quasi equal populated districts) or to the State people (quasi equal populated districts).

The "reserved power clause" may be applied in the following two ways:

Add bills through the State legislature where the 60-40 voting prevails counting the number of voting legislature members.

Add bills through the State people voting within "quasi equal populated districts" where the 60%-40% rule prevails of counting the number of winning "quasi equal populated districts" must be in forced to add a state bill.

The "reserved power clause" is based upon the "power of representation" within "quasi equal populate districts." Any judgment against the State bill violates the "power of representation" within the State people "quasi equal populated districts."

Constitution

Bill of Rights

10th Amendment

Delegated Clause (Constant)

Reserved Power Clause (Add Country Bill)

Add County Amendment

(A County Government Has the Power to Add a bill)

The 10th Amendment states "the powers (County) not delegated to the United States by the Constitution, nor prohibited by it (Constitution) to the Counties (legislature), are reserved (reserved power clause) to the Counties (legislature) respectively, or to the County people (quasi equal populated districts)."

In other words, "the powers (County) not delegated to the United States by the Constitution, or not prohibited (not allowed) by it (Constitution) to the Counties (legislature), are reserved (reserved power clause) to the Counties (legislature) respectively, or to the County people (quasi equal populated districts)."

In other words, "the powers (County) not delegated to the United States by the Constitution, or not allowed by it (Constitution) to the Counties (legislature), are reserved (reserved power clause) to

the Counties (legislature) respectively, or to the County people (quasi equal populated districts)."

In other words, "the powers (County) not delegated to the United States by the Constitution, or allowed by it (Constitution) to the Counties (legislature), are reserved (reserved power clause) to the Counties (legislature) respectively, or to the County people (quasi equal populated districts)."

The "reserved power clause" applies to the County legislature (quasi equal populated districts) or to the County people (quasi equal populated districts).

The "reserved power clause" may be applied in the following two ways:

Add bills through the County legislature where the 60-40 voting prevails counting the number of voting legislature members.

Add bills through the County people voting within "quasi equal populated districts" where the 60%-40% rule prevails of counting the number of winning "quasi equal populated districts" must be in forced.

The "reserved power clause" is based upon the "power of representation" within the County "quasi equal populate districts." Any judgment against the County bill violates the "power of representation" within the County people "quasi equal populated districts."

Constitution

Bill of Rights

10th Amendment

Delegated Clause (Constant)

Reserved Power Clause (Add City Bill)

ADD CITY BILL

(A City Government Has the Power to Add a Bill.)

The 10th Amendment states "the powers (City) not delegated to the United States by the Constitution, nor prohibited by it (Constitution) to the Cities (council), are reserved (reserved power clause) to the Cities (council) respectively, or to the city people (quasi equal populated districts)."

In other words, "the powers (City) not delegated to the United States by the Constitution, or not prohibited (not allowed) by it (Constitution) to the Cities (council), are reserved (reserved power clause) to the Cities (council) respectively, or to the city people (quasi equal populated districts)."

In other words, "the powers (City) not delegated to the United States by the Constitution, or not allowed by it (Constitution) to the Cities (council), are reserved (reserved power clause) to the

Cities (council) respectively, or to the city people (quasi equal populated districts)."

In other words, "the powers (City) not delegated to the United States by the Constitution, or allowed by it (Constitution) to the Cities (council), are reserved (reserved power clause) to the Cities (council) respectively, or to the city people (quasi equal populated districts)."

The "reserved power clause" applies to the city council (quasi equal populated districts) or to the city people (quasi equal populated districts).

The "reserved power clause" may be applied in the following two ways:

Add bills through the city council where the 60-40 voting prevails counting the number of voting legislature members.

Add bills through the City people voting within "quasi equal populated districts" where the 60%-40% rule prevails of counting the number of winning "quasi equal populated

districts" must be in forced.

The "reserved power clause" is based upon the "power of representation" within the City "quasi equal populate districts." Any judgment against the city bill violates the "power of representation" within the city people "quasi equal populated districts."

Constitution

Bill of Rights

10th Amendment

Delegated Clause (Constant)

Reserved Power Clause (Add Town Bill)

ADD TOWN BILL

(A Town Government Has the Power to Add a Bill.)

The 10th Amendment states "the powers (Town) not delegated to the United States by the Constitution, nor prohibited by it (Constitution) to the Towns (council), are reserved (reserved power clause) to the Towns (council) respectively, or to the Town people (quasi equal populated districts)."

In other words, "the powers (Town) not delegated to the United States by the Constitution, or not prohibited (not allowed) by it (Constitution) to the Towns (council), are reserved (reserved power clause) to the Towns (council) respectively, or to the Town people (quasi equal populated districts)."

In other words, "the powers (Town) not delegated to the United States by the Constitution, or not allowed by it (Constitution) to the Towns (council), are reserved (reserved power clause) to the

Towns (council) respectively, or to the Town people (quasi equal populated districts)."

In other words, "the powers (Town) not delegated to the United States by the Constitution, or allowed by it (Constitution) to the Towns (council), are reserved (reserved power clause) to the Towns (council) respectively, or to the Town people (quasi equal populated districts)."

The "reserved power clause" applies to the Town council (quasi equal populated districts) or to the Town people (quasi equal populated districts).

The "reserved power clause" may be applied in the following two ways: Add bills through the Town council where the 60-40 voting prevails counting the number of voting legislature members.

Add bills through the Town people voting within "quasi equal populated districts" where the 60%-40% rule prevails of counting the number of winning "quasi equal populated districts" must be in forced.

The "reserved power clause" is based upon the "power of representation" within the Town "quasi equal populate districts." Any judgment against the Town bill violates the "power of representation" within the Town people "quasi equal populated districts."

Constitution

Bill of Rights

10th Amendment

Delegated Clause (Constant)

Reserved Power Clause (Add Village Bill)

ADD VILLAGE BILL

(A Village Government Has the Power to Add a Bill.)

The 10th Amendment states "the powers (Village) not delegated to the United States by the Constitution, nor prohibited by it (Constitution) to the Villages (council), are reserved (reserved power clause) to the Villages (council) respectively, or to the Village people (quasi equal populated districts)."

In other words, "the powers (Village) not delegated to the United States by the Constitution, or not prohibited (not allowed) by it (Constitution) to the Villages (council), are reserved (reserved power clause) to the Villages (council) respectively, or to the Village people (quasi equal populated districts)."

In other words, "the powers (Village) not delegated to the United States by the Constitution, or not allowed by it (Constitution) to the Villages (council), are reserved (reserved power clause) to the

Villages (council) respectively, or to the Village people (quasi equal populated districts)."

In other words, "the powers (Village) not delegated to the United States by the Constitution, or allowed by it (Constitution) to the Villages (council), are reserved (reserved power clause) to the Villages (council) respectively, or to the Village people (quasi equal populated districts)."

The "reserved power clause" applies to the Village council (quasi equal populated districts) or to the Village people (quasi equal populated districts).

The "reserved power clause" may be applied in the following two ways: Add bills through the Village council where the 60-40 voting prevails counting the number of voting legislature members.

Add bills through the Village people voting within "quasi equal populated districts" where the 60%-40% rule prevails of counting the number of winning "quasi equal populated districts" must be in forced.

The "reserved power clause" is based upon the "power of representation" within the Village "quasi equal populate districts." Any judgment against the Village bill violates the "power of representation" within the Village people "quasi equal populated districts."

Constitution

Bill of Rights

10th Amendment

Delegated Clause (Constant)
Reserved Power Clause (Add House Bill)

ADD HOUSE BILL

(A House Government Has the Power to Add a Bill.)

The 10th Amendment states "the powers (House) not delegated to the United States by the Constitution, nor prohibited by it (Constitution) to the Houses (legislature), are reserved (reserved power clause) to the Houses (legislature) respectively, or to the House people (quasi equal populated districts)."

In other words, "the powers (House) not delegated to the United States by the Constitution, or not prohibited (not allowed) by it (Constitution) to the Houses (legislature), are reserved (reserved power clause) to the Houses (legislature) respectively, or to the House people (quasi equal populated districts)."

In other words, "the powers (House) not delegated to the United States by the Constitution, or not allowed by it (Constitution) to the Houses (legislature), are reserved (reserved power clause) to

the Houses (legislature) respectively, or to the House people (quasi equal populated districts)."

In other words, "the powers (House) not delegated to the United States by the Constitution, or allowed by it (Constitution) to the Houses (legislature), are reserved (reserved power clause) to the Houses (legislature) respectively, or to the House people (quasi equal populated districts)."

The "reserved power clause" applies to the House legislature (quasi equal populated districts) or to the House people (quasi equal populated districts).

The "reserved power clause" may be applied in the following two ways: Add bills through the House legislature where the 60-40 voting prevails counting the number of voting legislature members.

Add bills through the House people voting within "quasi equal populated districts" where the 60%-40% rule prevails of counting the number of winning "quasi equal populated districts" must be in forced.

The "reserved power clause" is based upon the "power of representation" within the House "quasi equal populate districts." Any judgment against the House bill violates the "power of representation" within the House people "quasi equal populated districts."

"Reserved Power Clause"

Rescind

Amendments

(State, County, City, Town, Village House)

Constitution

Bill of Rights

10th Amendment

Delegated Clause (Constant)

Reserved Power Clause (Rescind State Amendment)

RESCIND STATE AMENDMENT

(A State Government Has the Power to Rescind an Amendment.)

The 10th Amendment states "the powers (State) not delegated to the United States by the Constitution, nor prohibited by it (Constitution) to the States (legislature), are reserved (reserved power clause) to the States (legislature) respectively, or to the State people (quasi equal populated districts)."

In other words, "the powers (State) not delegated to the United States by the Constitution, or not prohibited (not allowed) by it (Constitution) to the States (legislature), are reserved (reserved power clause) to the States (legislature) respectively, or to the State people (quasi equal populated districts)."

In other words, "the powers (State) not delegated to the United States by the Constitution, or not allowed by it (Constitution) to the States (legislature), are reserved (reserved power clause) to the

States (legislature) respectively, or to the State people (quasi equal populated districts)."

In other words, "the powers (State) not delegated to the United States by the Constitution, or allowed by it (Constitution) to the States (legislature), are reserved (reserved power clause) to the States (legislature) respectively, or to the State people (quasi equal populated districts)."

The "reserved power clause" applies to the State legislature (quasi equal populated districts) or to the State people (quasi equal populated districts).

The "reserved power clause" may be applied in the following two ways:

Rescind amendments through the State legislature where the 60-40 voting prevails counting the number of voting legislature members.

Rescind amendments through the State people voting within "quasi equal populated districts" where the 60%-40% rule prevails of counting the number of winning "quasi equal populated districts" must be in forced to rescind a state amendment.

The "reserved power clause" is based upon the "power of representation" within "quasi equal populate districts." Any judgment against the State rescind amendment violates the "power of representation" within the State people "quasi equal populated districts.

Constitution

Bill of Rights

10th Amendment

Delegated Clause (Constant)
Reserved Power Clause (Rescind County Amendment)

RESCIND COUNTY AMENDMENT

(A County Government Has the Power to Rescind an Amendment.)

The 10th Amendment states "the powers (County) not delegated to the United States by the Constitution, nor prohibited by it (Constitution) to the Counties (legislature), are reserved (reserved power clause) to the Counties (legislature) respectively, or to the County people (quasi equal populated districts)."

In other words, "the powers (County) not delegated to the United States by the Constitution, or not prohibited (not allowed) by it (Constitution) to the Counties (legislature), are reserved (reserved power clause) to the Counties (legislature) respectively, or to the County people (quasi equal populated districts)."

In other words, "the powers (County) not delegated to the United States by the Constitution, or not allowed by it (Constitution) to the Counties (legislature), are reserved (reserved power clause) to

the Counties (legislature) respectively, or to the County people (quasi equal populated districts)." In other words, "the powers (County) not delegated to the United States by the Constitution, or allowed by it (Constitution) to the Counties (legislature), are reserved (reserved power clause) to the Counties (legislature) respectively, or to the County people (quasi equal populated districts)."

The "reserved power clause" applies to the County legislature (quasi equal populated districts) or to the County people (quasi equal populated districts).

The "reserved power clause" may be applied in the following two ways:

Rescind amendments through the County legislature where the 60-40 voting prevails counting the number of voting legislature members.

Rescind amendments through the County people voting within "quasi equal populated districts" where the 60%- 40% rule prevails of counting the number of winning "quasi equal populated districts" must be in forced.

The "reserved power clause" is based upon the "power of representation" within the County "quasi equal populate districts." Any judgment against the County rescind amendment violates the "power of representation" within the County people "quasi equal populated districts."

Constitution

Bill of Rights

10th Amendment

Delegated Clause (Constant)

Reserved Power Clause (Rescind City Amendment)

RESCIND CITYAMENDMENT

(A City Government Has the Power to Rescind an Amendment.)

The 10th Amendment states "the powers (City) not delegated to the United States by the Constitution, nor prohibited by it (Constitution) to the Cities (council), are reserved (reserved power clause) to the Cities (council) respectively, or to the city people (quasi equal populated districts)."

In other words, "the powers (City) not delegated to the United States by the Constitution, or not prohibited (not allowed) by it (Constitution) to the Cities (council), are reserved (reserved power clause) to the Cities (council) respectively, or to the city people (quasi equal populated districts)."

In other words, "the powers (City) not delegated to the United States by the Constitution, or not allowed by it (Constitution) to the Cities (council), are reserved (reserved power clause) to the

Cities (council) respectively, or to the city people (quasi equal populated districts)."

In other words, "the powers (City) not delegated to the United States by the Constitution, or allowed by it (Constitution) to the Cities (council), are reserved (reserved power clause) to the Cities (council) respectively, or to the city people (quasi equal populated districts)."

The "reserved power clause" applies to the city council (quasi equal populated districts) or to the city people (quasi equal populated districts).

The "reserved power clause" may be applied in the following two ways:

Rescind amendments through the city council where the 60-40 voting prevails counting the number of voting legislature members.

Rescind amendments through the City people voting within "quasi equal populated districts" where the 60%-40% rule prevails of counting the number of winning "quasi equal populated districts" must be in forced. The "reserved power clause" is based upon the "power of representation" within the City "quasi equal populate districts." Any judgment against the city rescind amendment violates the "power of representation" within the city people "quasi equal populated districts."

Constitution

Bill of Rights

10th Amendment

Delegated Clause (Constant)

Reserved Power Clause (Rescind Town Amendment)

RESCIND TOWN AMENDMENT

(A Town Government Has the Power to Rescind an Amendment.)

The 10th Amendment states "the powers (Town) not delegated to the United States by the Constitution, nor prohibited by it (Constitution) to the Towns (council), are reserved (reserved power clause) to the Towns (council) respectively, or to the Town people (quasi equal populated districts)."

In other words, "the powers (Town) not delegated to the United States by the Constitution, or not prohibited (not allowed) by it (Constitution) to the Towns (council), are reserved (reserved power clause) to the Towns (council) respectively, or to the Town people (quasi equal populated districts)."

In other words, "the powers (Town) not delegated to the United States by the Constitution, or not allowed by it (Constitution) to the Towns (council), are reserved (reserved power clause) to the

Towns (council) respectively, or to the Town people (quasi equal populated districts)."

In other words, "the powers (Town) not delegated to the United States by the Constitution, or allowed by it (Constitution) to the Towns (council), are reserved (reserved power clause) to the Towns (council) respectively, or to the Town people (quasi equal populated districts)."

The "reserved power clause" applies to the Town council (quasi equal populated districts) or to the Town people (quasi equal populated districts).

The "reserved power clause" may be applied in the following two ways:

Rescind amendments through the Town council where the 60-40 voting prevails counting the number of voting legislature members.

Rescind amendments through the Town people voting within "quasi equal populated districts" where the 60%-40% rule prevails of counting the number of winning "quasi equal populated districts" must be in forced.

The "reserved power clause" is based upon the "power of representation" within the Town "quasi equal populate districts." Any judgment against the Town rescind amendment violates the "power of representation" within the Town people "quasi equal populated districts."

Constitution

Bill of Rights

10th Amendment

Delegated Clause (Constant)

Reserved Power Clause (Rescind Village Amendment)

RESCIND VILLAGE AMENDMENT

(A Village Government Has the Power to Rescind an Amendment.)

The 10th Amendment states "the powers (Village) not delegated to the United States by the Constitution, nor prohibited by it (Constitution) to the Villages (council), are reserved (reserved power clause) to the Villages (council) respectively, or to the Village people (quasi equal populated districts)."

In other words, "the powers (Village) not delegated to the United States by the Constitution, or not prohibited (not allowed) by it (Constitution) to the Villages (council), are reserved (reserved power clause) to the Villages (council) respectively, or to the Village people (quasi equal populated districts)."

In other words, "the powers (Village) not delegated to the United States by the Constitution, or not allowed by it (Constitution) to the Villages (council), are reserved (reserved power clause) to the

Villages (council) respectively, or to the Village people (quasi equal populated districts)."

In other words, "the powers (Village) not delegated to the United States by the Constitution, or allowed by it (Constitution) to the Villages (council), are reserved (reserved power clause) to the Villages (council) respectively, or to the Village people (quasi equal populated districts)."

The "reserved power clause" applies to the Village council (quasi equal populated districts) or to the Village people (quasi equal populated districts).

The "reserved power clause" may be applied in the following two ways: Rescind amendments through the Village council where the 60-40 voting prevails counting the number of voting legislature members. Rescind amendments through the Village people voting within "quasi equal populated districts" where the 60%-40% rule prevails of counting the number of winning "quasi equal populated districts" must be in forced.

The "reserved power clause" is based upon the "power of representation" within the Village "quasi equal populate districts." Any judgment against the Village rescinds amendment violates the "power of representation" within the Village people "quasi equal populated districts."

"Reserved Power Clause"

Rescind Bills

(State, County, City, Town, Village House)

Constitution

Bill of Rights

10th Amendment

Delegated Clause (Constant)
Reserved Power Clause (Rescind State Bill)

RESCIND STATE BILL
(A State Government Has the Power to Rescind a Bill.)

The 10th Bill states "the powers (State) not delegated to the United States by the Constitution, nor prohibited by it (Constitution) to the States (legislature), are reserved (reserved power clause) to the States (legislature) respectively, or to the State people (quasi equal populated districts)."

In other words, "the powers (State) not delegated to the United States by the Constitution, or not prohibited (not allowed) by it (Constitution) to the States (legislature), are reserved (reserved power clause) to the States (legislature) respectively, or to the State people (quasi equal populated districts)."

In other words, "the powers (State) not delegated to the United States by the Constitution, or not allowed by it (Constitution) to the States (legislature), are reserved (reserved power clause) to the

States (legislature) respectively, or to the State people (quasi equal populated districts)."

In other words, "the powers (State) not delegated to the United States by the Constitution, or allowed by it (Constitution) to the States (legislature), are reserved (reserved power clause) to the States (legislature) respectively, or to the State people (quasi equal populated districts)."

The "reserved power clause" applies to the State legislature (quasi equal populated districts) or to the State people (quasi equal populated districts).

The "reserved power clause" may be applied in the following two ways:

Rescind bills through the State legislature where the 60-40 voting prevails counting the number of voting legislature members. Rescind bills through the State people voting within "quasi equal populated districts" where the 60%-40% rule prevails of counting the number of winning "quasi equal populated districts" must be in forced to rescind a state bill.

The "reserved power clause" is based upon the "power of representation" within "quasi equal populate districts." Any judgment against the State rescind bill violates the "power of representation" within the State people "quasi equal populated districts."

Constitution

Bill of Rights

10th Amendment

Delegated Clause (Constant)

Reserved Power Clause (Rescind County Bill)

RESCIND COUNTY BILL

(A County Government Has the Power to Rescind a Bill.)

The 10th Bill states "the powers (County) not delegated to the United States by the Constitution, nor prohibited by it (Constitution) to the Counties (legislature), are reserved (reserved power clause) to the Counties (legislature) respectively, or to the County people (quasi equal populated districts)."

In other words, "the powers (County) not delegated to the United States by the Constitution, or not prohibited (not allowed) by it (Constitution) to the Counties (legislature), are reserved (reserved power clause) to the Counties (legislature) respectively, or to the County people (quasi equal populated districts)."

In other words, "the powers (County) not delegated to the United States by the Constitution, or not allowed by it (Constitution) to the Counties (legislature), are reserved (reserved power clause) to

the Counties (legislature) respectively, or to the County people (quasi equal populated districts)."

In other words, "the powers (County) not delegated to the United States by the Constitution, or allowed by it (Constitution) to the Counties (legislature), are reserved (reserved power clause) to the Counties (legislature) respectively, or to the County people (quasi equal populated districts)."

The "reserved power clause" applies to the County legislature (quasi equal populated districts) or to the County people (quasi equal populated districts).

The "reserved power clause" may be applied in the following two ways:

Rescind bills through the County legislature where the 60-40 voting prevails counting the number of voting legislature members.

Rescind bills through the County people voting within "quasi equal populated districts" where the 60%-40% rule prevails of counting the number of winning "quasi equal populated districts" must be in forced. The "reserved power clause" is based upon the "power of representation" within the County "quasi equal populate districts." Any judgment against the County rescind bill violates the "power of representation" within the County people "quasi equal populated districts."

Constitution

Bill of Rights

10th Amendment

Delegated Clause (Constant)
Reserved Power Clause (Rescind City Bill)

RESCIND CITY BILL

(A City Government Has the Power to Rescind a Bill.)

The 10th Bill states "the powers (City) not delegated to the United States by the Constitution, nor prohibited by it (Constitution) to the Cities (council), are reserved (reserved power clause) to the Cities (council) respectively, or to the city people (quasi equal populated districts)."

In other words, "the powers (City) not delegated to the United States by the Constitution, or not prohibited (not allowed) by it (Constitution) to the Cities (council), are reserved (reserved power clause) to the Cities (council) respectively, or to the city people (quasi equal populated districts)."

In other words, "the powers (City) not delegated to the United States by the Constitution, or not allowed by it (Constitution) to the Cities (council), are reserved (reserved power clause) to the

Cities (council) respectively, or to the city people (quasi equal populated districts)."

In other words, "the powers (City) not delegated to the United States by the Constitution, or allowed by it (Constitution) to the Cities (council), are reserved (reserved power clause) to the Cities (council) respectively, or to the city people (quasi equal populated districts)."

The "reserved power clause" applies to the city council (quasi equal populated districts) or to the city people (quasi equal populated districts).

The "reserved power clause" may be applied in the following two ways:

Rescind bills through the city council where the 60-40 voting prevails counting the number of voting legislature members. Rescind bills through the City people voting within "quasi equal populated districts" where the 60%-40% rule prevails of counting the number of winning "quasi equal populated districts" must be in forced.

The "reserved power clause" is based upon the "power of representation" within the City "quasi equal populate districts." Any judgment against the city rescind bill violates the "power of representation" within the city people "quasi equal populated districts."

Constitution

Bill of Rights

10th Amendment

Delegated Clause (Constant)

Reserved Power Clause (Rescind Town Bill)

RESCIND TOWN BILL

(A Town Government Has the Power to Rescind a Bill.)

The 10th Bill states "the powers (Town) not delegated to the United States by the Constitution, nor prohibited by it (Constitution) to the Towns (council), are reserved (reserved power clause) to the Towns (council) respectively, or to the Town people (quasi equal populated districts)."

In other words, "the powers (Town) not delegated to the United States by the Constitution, or not prohibited (not allowed) by it (Constitution) to the Towns (council), are reserved (reserved power clause) to the Towns (council) respectively, or to the Town people (quasi equal populated districts)."

In other words, "the powers (Town) not delegated to the United States by the Constitution, or not allowed by it (Constitution) to the Towns (council), are reserved (reserved power clause) to the

Towns (council) respectively, or to the Town people (quasi equal populated districts)."

In other words, "the powers (Town) not delegated to the United States by the Constitution, or allowed by it (Constitution) to the Towns (council), are reserved (reserved power clause) to the Towns (council) respectively, or to the Town people (quasi equal populated districts)."

The "reserved power clause" applies to the Town council (quasi equal populated districts) or to the Town people (quasi equal populated districts).

The "reserved power clause" may be applied in the following two ways:

Rescind bills through the Town council where the 60-40 voting prevails counting the number of voting legislature members. Rescind bills through the Town people voting within "quasi equal populated districts" where the 60%-40% rule prevails of counting the number of winning "quasi equal populated districts" must be in forced.

The "reserved power clause" is based upon the "power of representation" within the Town "quasi equal populate districts." Any judgment against the Town rescind bill violates the "power of representation" within the Town people "quasi equal populated districts."

Constitution

Bill of Rights

10th Amendment

Delegated Clause (Constant)
Reserved Power Clause (Rescind Village Bill)

RESCIND VILLAGE BILL

(A Village Government Has the Power to Rescind a Bill.)

The 10th Bill states "the powers (Village) not delegated to the United States by the Constitution, nor prohibited by it (Constitution) to the Villages (council), are reserved (reserved power clause) to the Villages (council) respectively, or to the Village people (quasi equal populated districts)."

In other words, "the powers (Village) not delegated to the United States by the Constitution, or not prohibited (not allowed) by it (Constitution) to the Villages (council), are reserved (reserved power clause) to the Villages (council) respectively, or to the Village people (quasi equal populated districts)."

In other words, "the powers (Village) not delegated to the United States by the Constitution, or not allowed by it (Constitution) to the Villages (council), are reserved (reserved power clause) to the

Villages (council) respectively, or to the Village people (quasi equal populated districts)."

In other words, "the powers (Village) not delegated to the United States by the Constitution, or allowed by it (Constitution) to the Villages (council), are reserved (reserved power clause) to the Villages (council) respectively, or to the Village people (quasi equal populated districts)."

The "reserved power clause" applies to the Village council (quasi equal populated districts) or to the Village people (quasi equal populated districts).

The "reserved power clause" may be applied in the following two ways:

Rescind bills through the Village council where the 60-40 voting prevails counting the number of voting legislature members. Rescind bills through the Village people voting within "quasi equal populated districts" where the 60%-40% rule prevails of counting the number of winning "quasi equal populated districts" must be in forced.

The "reserved power clause" is based upon the "power of representation" within the Village "quasi equal populate districts." Any judgment against the Village rescind bill violates the "power of representation" within the Village people "quasi equal populated districts."

Executive Orders and Power of Representation Nullification

State Governor Order nullifies the **State power of representation** within **quasi equal populated districts.**

Impeach State Governor.

County Executive Order nullifies the **County power of representation** within **quasi equal populated districts.**

Impeach County Executive.

City Mayor Order nullifies the **city power of representation** within **quasi equal populated districts.**

Impeach City Mayor.

Town Mayor Order nullifies the **Town power of representation** within **quasi equal populated districts.**

Impeach Town Mayor.

Village Mayor Order nullifies the **Village power of representation** within **quasi equal populated districts.**

Impeach Village Mayor.

“Reserved Power Clause”

Impeach

(State Governor, County Executive, City Mayor, Town Mayor, Village Mayor, House Leader)

Constitution

Bill of Rights

10th Amendment

Delegated Clause (Constant)

Reserved Power Clause (Impeach State Governor)

IMPEACH STATE GOVERNOR

(Remove State Governor)

The 10th Amendment states "the powers (State) not delegated to the United States by the Constitution, nor prohibited by it (Constitution) to the States (legislature), are reserved (reserved power clause) to the States (legislature) respectively, or to the State people (quasi equal populated districts)."

In other words, "the powers (State) not delegated to the United States by the Constitution, or not prohibited (not allowed) by it (Constitution) to the States (legislature), are reserved (reserved power clause) to the States (legislature) respectively, or to the State people (quasi equal populated districts)."

In other words, "the powers (State) not delegated to the United States by the Constitution, or not allowed by it (Constitution) to the States (legislature), are reserved (reserved power clause) to the

States (legislature) respectively, or to the State people (quasi equal populated districts)."

In other words, "the powers (State) not delegated to the United States by the Constitution, or allowed by it (Constitution) to the States (legislature), are reserved (reserved power clause) to the States (legislature) respectively, or to the State people (quasi equal populated districts)." The "reserved power clause" applies to the State legislature (quasi equal populated districts) or to the State people. (quasi equal populated districts).

The "reserved power clause" may be applied in the following two ways:

Impeach governor through the State legislature members voting enforcing 60%-40% rule.

Impeach governor through the State people voting in "quasi equal populated districts" enforcing the 60%-40% rule on the winning districts.

The "reserved power clause" is based upon the "power of representation" within State "quasi equal populate districts." Any judgment against the impeach State governor violates the "power of representation" within the State people "quasi equal populated districts."

Constitution

Bill of Rights

10th Amendment

Delegated Clause (Constant)

Reserved Power Clause (Impeach County Executive)

IMPEACH COUNTY EXECUTIVE

(Remove County Executive)

The 10th Amendment states "the powers (County) not delegated to the United States by the Constitution, nor prohibited by it (Constitution) to the Counties (legislature), are reserved (reserved power clause) to the Counties (legislature) respectively, or to the County people (quasi equal populated districts)."

In other words, "the powers (County) not delegated to the United States by the Constitution, or not prohibited (not allowed) by it (Constitution) to the Counties (legislature), are reserved (reserved power clause) to the Counties (legislature) respectively, or to the County people (quasi equal populated districts)."

In other words, "the powers (County) not delegated to the United States by the Constitution, or not allowed by it (Constitution) to the Counties (legislature), are reserved (reserved power clause) to

the Counties (legislature) respectively, or to the County people (quasi equal populated districts)."

In other words, "the powers (County) not delegated to the United States by the Constitution, or allowed by it (Constitution) to the Counties (legislature), are reserved (reserved power clause) to the Counties (legislature) respectively, or to the County people (quasi equal populated districts)."

The "reserved power clause" applies to the County legislature (quasi equal populated districts) or to the County people (quasi equal populated districts).

The "reserved power clause" may be applied in the following two ways:

Impeach County executive through the County legislature members voting enforcing 60%-40% rule.

Impeach County executive through the County people voting in "quasi equal populated districts" enforcing the 60%-40% rule on the winning districts.

The "reserved power clause" is based upon the "power of representation" within County "quasi equal populate districts." Any judgment against impeach County executive violates the "power of representation" within the County people "quasi equal populated districts."

Constitution

Bill of Rights

10th Amendment

Delegated Clause (Constant)
Reserved Power Clause (Impeach City Mayor)

IMPEACH CITY MAYOR

(Remove City Mayor)

The 10th Amendment states "the powers (City) not delegated to the United States by the Constitution, nor prohibited by it (Constitution) to the Cities (council), are reserved (reserved power clause) to the Cities (council) respectively, or to the city people (quasi equal populated districts)."

In other words, "the powers (City) not delegated to the United States by the Constitution, or not prohibited (not allowed) by it (Constitution) to the Cities (council), are reserved (reserved power clause) to the Cities (council) respectively, or to the city people (quasi equal populated districts)."

In other words, "the powers (City) not delegated to the United States by the Constitution, or not allowed by it (Constitution) to the Cities (council), are reserved (reserved power clause) to the

Cities (council) respectively, or to the city people (quasi equal populated districts)."

In other words, "the powers (City) not delegated to the United States by the Constitution, or allowed by it (Constitution) to the Cities (council), are reserved (reserved power clause) to the Cities (council) respectively, or to the city people (quasi equal populated districts)."

The "reserved power clause" applies to the city council (quasi equal populated districts) or to the city people (quasi equal populated districts).

The "reserved power clause" may be applied in the following two ways:

Impeach City mayor through the City council members voting enforcing 60%-40% rule.

Impeach City mayor through the City people voting in "quasi equal populated districts" enforcing the 60%-40% rule on the winning districts.

The "reserved power clause" is based upon the "power of representation" within City "quasi equal populate districts." Any judgment against the impeach City mayor violates the "power of representation" within the city people "quasi equal populated districts."

Constitution

Bill of Rights

10th Amendment

Delegated Clause (Constant)
Reserved Power Clause (Impeach Town Mayor)

IMPEACH TOWN MAYOR
(Remove Town Mayor)

The 10th Amendment states "the powers (Town) not delegated to the United States by the Constitution, nor prohibited by it (Constitution) to the Towns (council), are reserved (reserved power clause) to the Towns (council) respectively, or to the Town people (quasi equal populated districts)."

In other words, "the powers (Town) not delegated to the United States by the Constitution, or not prohibited (not allowed) by it (Constitution) to the Towns (council), are reserved (reserved power clause) to the Towns (council) respectively, or to the Town people (quasi equal populated districts)."

In other words, "the powers (Town) not delegated to the United States by the Constitution, or not allowed by it (Constitution) to the Towns (council), are reserved (reserved power clause) to the

Towns (council) respectively, or to the Town people (quasi equal populated districts)."

In other words, "the powers (Town) not delegated to the United States by the Constitution, or allowed by it (Constitution) to the Towns (council), are reserved (reserved power clause) to the Towns (council) respectively, or to the Town people (quasi equal populated districts)."

The "reserved power clause" applies to the Town council (quasi equal populated districts) or to the Town people (quasi equal populated districts).

The "reserved power clause" may be applied in the following two ways:

Impeach Town mayor through the Town council members voting enforcing 60%-40% rule.

Impeach Town mayor through the Town people voting in "quasi equal populated districts" enforcing the 60%-40% rule on the winning districts.

The "reserved power clause" is based upon the "power of representation" within Town "quasi equal populate districts." Any judgment against the impeach Town mayor violates the "power of representation" within the Town people "quasi equal populated districts."

Constitution

Bill of Rights

10th Amendment

Delegated Clause (Constant)
Reserved Power Clause (Impeach Village Mayor)

IMPEACH Village Mayor
(Remove Village Mayor)

The 10th Amendment states "the powers (Village) not delegated to the United States by the Constitution, nor prohibited by it (Constitution) to the Villages (council), are reserved (reserved power clause) to the Villages (council) respectively, or to the Village people (quasi equal populated districts)."

In other words, "the powers (Village) not delegated to the United States by the Constitution, or not prohibited (not allowed) by it (Constitution) to the Villages (council), are reserved (reserved power clause) to the Villages (council) respectively, or to the Village people (quasi equal populated districts)."

In other words, "the powers (Village) not delegated to the United States by the Constitution, or not allowed by it (Constitution) to the Villages (council), are reserved (reserved power clause) to the

Villages (council) respectively, or to the Village people (quasi equal populated districts)."

In other words, "the powers (Village) not delegated to the United States by the Constitution, or allowed by it (Constitution) to the Villages (council), are reserved (reserved power clause) to the Villages (council) respectively, or to the Village people (quasi equal populated districts)."

The "reserved power clause" applies to the Village council (quasi equal populated districts) or to the Village people (quasi equal populated districts).

The "reserved power clause" may be applied in the following two ways:

Impeach Village mayor through the Village council members voting enforcing 60%-40% rule.

Impeach Village mayor through the Village people voting in "quasi equal populated districts" enforcing the 60%- 40% rule on the winning districts.

The "reserved power clause" is based upon the "power of representation" within Village "quasi equal populate districts." Any judgment against the impeach Village mayor violates the "power of representation" within the Village people "quasi equal

populated districts."

Constitution

Bill of Rights

10th Amendment

Delegated Clause (Constant)

Reserved Power Clause (Impeach House Leader)

IMPEACH HOUSE LEADER

(Remove House Leader)

The 10th Amendment states "the powers (House) not delegated to the United States by the Constitution, nor prohibited by it (Constitution) to the Houses (legislature), are reserved (reserved power clause) to the Houses (legislature) respectively, or to the House people (quasi equal populated districts)."

In other words, "the powers (House) not delegated to the United States by the Constitution, or not prohibited (not allowed) by it (Constitution) to the Houses (legislature), are reserved (reserved power clause) to the Houses (legislature) respectively, or to the House people (quasi equal populated districts)."

In other words, "the powers (House) not delegated to the United States by the Constitution, or not allowed by it (Constitution) to the Houses (legislature), are reserved (reserved power clause) to

the Houses (legislature) respectively, or to the House people (quasi equal populated districts)."

In other words, "the powers (House) not delegated to the United States by the Constitution, or allowed by it (Constitution) to the Houses (legislature), are reserved (reserved power clause) to the Houses (legislature) respectively, or to the House people (quasi equal populated districts)."

The "reserved power clause" applies to the House legislature (quasi equal populated districts) or to the House people (quasi equal populated districts).

The "reserved power clause" may be applied in the following two ways:

Impeach house leader through the House legislature members voting enforcing 60%-40% rule.

Impeach house leader through the House people voting in "quasi equal populated districts" enforcing the 60%-40% rule on the winning districts.

The "reserved power clause" is based upon the "power of representation" within House "quasi equal populate districts." Any judgment against the impeach house leader violates the "power of representation" within the House people "quasi equal populated districts."

“Reserved Power Clause”

Impeach

(United States Senator, United States President, President Cabinet Members, United States Judge)

Constitution

Bill of Rights

10th Amendment

Delegated Clause (Constant)

Reserved Power Clause (Impeach US Senator)

IMPEACH UNITED STATES SENATOR

(Remove a United States Senator)

The 10th Amendment states "the powers (State) not delegated to the United States by the Constitution, nor prohibited by it (Constitution) to the States (legislature), are reserved (reserved power clause) to the States (legislature) respectively, or to the State people (quasi equal populated districts)."

In other words, "the powers (State) not delegated to the United States by the Constitution, or not prohibited (not allowed) by it (Constitution) to the States (legislature), are reserved (reserved power clause) to the States (legislature) respectively, or to the State people (quasi equal populated districts)."

In other words, "the powers (State) not delegated to the United States by the Constitution, or not allowed by it (Constitution) to the States (legislature), are reserved (reserved power clause) to the

States (legislature) respectively, or to the State people (quasi equal populated districts)."

In other words, "the powers (State) not delegated to the United States by the Constitution, or allowed by it (Constitution) to the States (legislature), are reserved (reserved power clause) to the States (legislature) respectively, or to the State people (quasi equal populated districts)."

The "reserved power clause" applies to the State legislature (quasi equal populated districts) or to the State people (quasi equal populated districts).

The "reserved power clause" may be applied in the following two ways:

Impeach a United States senator through the State legislature members voting enforcing 60%-40% rule.

Impeach a United States senator through the State people voting in "quasi equal populated districts" enforcing the 60%-40% rule on the winning districts.

The "reserved power clause" is based upon the "power of representation" within State "quasi equal populate districts." Any judgment against impeach a United States senator violates the "power of representation" within the State people "quasi equal populated districts."

Constitution

Bill of Rights

10th Amendment

Delegated Clause (Constant)

Reserved Power Clause (Impeach US President)

IMPEACH UNITED STATES PRESIDENT

(Remove a United States President)

The 10th Amendment states "the powers (State) not delegated to the United States by the Constitution, nor prohibited by it (Constitution) to the States (legislature), are reserved (reserved power clause) to the States (legislature) respectively, or to the State people (quasi equal populated districts)."

In other words, "the powers (State) not delegated to the United States by the Constitution, or not prohibited (not allowed) by it (Constitution) to the States (legislature), are reserved (reserved power clause) to the States (legislature) respectively, or to the State people (quasi equal populated districts)."

In other words, "the powers (State) not delegated to the United States by the Constitution, or not allowed by it (Constitution) to the States (legislature), are reserved (reserved power clause) to the

States (legislature) respectively, or to the State people (quasi equal populated districts)."

In other words, "the powers (State) not delegated to the United States by the Constitution, or allowed by it (Constitution) to the States (legislature), are reserved (reserved power clause) to the States (legislature) respectively, or to the State people (quasi equal populated districts)."

The "reserved power clause" applies to the State legislature (quasi equal populated districts) or to the State people (quasi equal populated districts).

The "reserved power clause" may be applied in the following two ways:

Impeach the President through the State legislature members voting enforcing 60%-40% rule.

Impeach the President through the State people voting in "quasi equal populated districts" enforcing the 60%-40% rule on the winning districts 75% of the States must agree to impeach a President in order to impeach a President.

The "reserved power clause" is based upon the "power of representation" within State "quasi equal populate districts." Any judgment against impeach President violates the "power of representation" within the State people "quasi equal populated districts."

Constitution

Bill of Rights

10th Amendment

Delegated Clause (Constant)
Reserved Power Clause (Impeach President Cabinet Members)

President Cabinet Members

- Vice President
- Department of State
- Department of the Treasury
- Department of Defense
- Department of Justice
- Department of the Interior
- Department of Agriculture
- Department of Commerce
- Department of Labor
- Department of Health and Human Services
- Department of Housing and Urban Development

- Department of Transportation
- Department of Energy
    - Secretary: Ernest Moniz
- Department of Education
- Department of Veterans Affairs
- Department of Homeland Security

IMPEACH UNITED STATES PRESIDENT CABINET MEMBER

(Remove a United States President cabinet member)

The 10th Amendment states "the powers (State) not delegated to the United States by the Constitution, nor prohibited by it (Constitution) to the States (legislature), are reserved (reserved power clause) to the States (legislature) respectively, or to the State people (quasi equal populated districts)."

In other words, "the powers (State) not delegated to the United States by the Constitution, or not prohibited (not allowed) by it (Constitution) to the States (legislature), are reserved (reserved power clause) to the States (legislature) respectively, or to the State people (quasi equal populated districts)."

In other words, "the powers (State) not delegated to the United States by the Constitution, or not allowed by it (Constitution) to the States (legislature), are reserved (reserved power clause) to the States (legislature) respectively, or to the State people (quasi equal populated districts)."

In other words, "the powers (State) not delegated to the United States by the Constitution, or allowed by it (Constitution) to the States (legislature), are reserved (reserved power clause) to the States (legislature) respectively, or to the State people (quasi equal populated districts)."

The "reserved power clause" applies to the State legislature (quasi equal populated districts) or to the State people (quasi equal populated districts).

The "reserved power clause" may be applied in the following two ways:

Impeach President cabinet member through the State legislature members voting enforcing 60%-40% rule.

Impeach President cabinet member through the State people voting in "quasi equal populated districts" enforcing the 60%-40% rule on the winning districts.

75% of the States must agree to impeach a United States President cabinet member in order to impeach a President cabinet member.

The "reserved power clause" is based upon the "power of representation" within State "quasi equal populate districts." Any judgment against the impeachment of a United States President cabinet member violates the "power of representation" within the State people "quasi equal populated districts."

Constitution

Bill of Rights

10th Amendment

Delegated Clause (Constant)
Reserved Power Clause (Impeach US Judge)

IMPEACH UNITED STATES JUDGE
(Remove a United States Judge)

The 10th Amendment states "the powers (State) not delegated to the United States by the Constitution, nor prohibited by it (Constitution) to the States (legislature), are reserved (reserved power clause) to the States (legislature) respectively, or to the State people (quasi equal populated districts)."

In other words, "the powers (State) not delegated to the United States by the Constitution, or not prohibited (not allowed) by it (Constitution) to the States (legislature), are reserved (reserved power clause) to the States (legislature) respectively, or to the State people (quasi equal populated districts)."

In other words, "the powers (State) not delegated to the United States by the Constitution, or not allowed by it (Constitution) to the States (legislature), are reserved (reserved power clause) to the

States (legislature) respectively, or to the State people (quasi equal populated districts)."

In other words, "the powers (State) not delegated to the United States by the Constitution, or allowed by it (Constitution) to the States (legislature), are reserved (reserved power clause) to the States (legislature) respectively, or to the State people (quasi equal populated districts)."

The "reserved power clause" applies to the State legislature (quasi equal populated districts) or to the State people (quasi equal populated districts).

The "reserved power clause" may be applied in the following two ways:

Impeach a United States Judge through the State legislature members voting enforcing 60%-40% rule.

Impeach a United States Judge through the State people voting in "quasi equal populated districts" enforcing the 60%-40% rule on the winning districts. 75% of the States must agree to impeach a United States Judge in order to impeach a United States Judge.

The "reserved power clause" is based upon the "power of representation" within State "quasi equal populate districts." Any judgment against impeach a United States Judge violates the "power of representation" within the State people "quasi equal populated districts."

SALES TAXES
(16th Amendment)

- **Company Sales Tax**
- **Healthcare Sales Tax**
- **IRS Sales Tax**
- **Social Security Sales Tax**
- **Medicare Sales Tax**
- **Unemployment Sales Tax**

COMPANY SALES TAX
(16th Amendment Multi tax)

Companies pay “Company tax” to the Federal Government and the market place as a sales tax as prescribed under the 16th Amendment.

Only Companies make money on products and services in the market place; therefore, all the products and services in the market will be tainted with the “Company sales tax.” Other Companies also passed “Company taxes” to the marketplace.

Companies use other companies to produce a product that the causes “Company sales tax” to snowball in the market place.

Both the Company and “Company snowball taxes” saturate products and services in the market place as sales taxes.

The Federal government collects the “Company tax” and takes a table percentage of the “Company sales tax” and “Company snowball sales tax.” The Federal government collects a triple multi tax made of “Company taxes,” “Company sales taxes” and “Company snowball sales tax.” The Federal government sales tax collections get hid- den (transparent) in the Treasury; whereas, the “Company taxes” get tabulated (known).

Any purchase made in the market place must pay both “Company sales tax” and Company snowball sales tax.”

COMPANY AND HEATH CARE SALES TAX
(16th Amendment Multi tax)

A Company sends the "Company tax" and "Health Care wage tax" to the Federal government as prescribed under the 16th Amendment.

The Company transfers "Company tax" and "Health Care wage tax" to the market place as sale taxes.

"Other Companies" sends their "Company tax" and "Health Care wage tax" to the Federal government. Companies use "other Companies" to produce a product that the causes "Health Care wage sales tax" and "Company sales tax" to snowball in the market place.

Only Companies make money on products and ser- vices in the market place; therefore, all the products and services in the market will be tainted with the "Health Care wage sales tax," "Health Care snowball wage sales tax," "Company sales tax," and "Company snowball sales tax." Any purchase made in the market place must pay the "Health Care wage sales tax," "Health Care snowball wage sales tax," "Company sales tax," and "Company snowball sales tax."

When making purchases in the market place, a "gross wage earner" who shelled out his "Health Care wage tax" to the Federal government pays also the "Health Care wage sales tax," "Health Care snowball wage sales tax," "Company sales tax" and

"Company snowball sales tax." The "gross wage earner" pays "Health Care wage tax" three times over and the "Company tax" two times over.

A non-wage earner is only exposed to the "Health Care wage sales tax," "Health Care snowball wage sales tax," "Company sales tax" and "Company snowball sales tax." The non-wage earner pays both the "Health Care wage tax" and Company tax two times over.

The Federal government collects the "gross wage earners" "Health Care wage tax" and takes a table percentage of the "Health Care wage sales tax," "Health Care snowball wage sales tax," "Company sales tax" and "Company snow- ball sales tax."

The Federal government sales tax collections get hid- den in the Treasury.

COMPANY AND IRS SALES TAX

(16th Amendment Multi tax)

A Company sends the "Company tax" and "IRS wage tax" to the Federal government as prescribed under the 16th Amendment.

The Company transfers "Company tax" and "IRS wage tax" to the market place as sale taxes.

"Other Companies" sends their "Company tax" and "IRS wage tax" to the Federal government. Companies use "other Companies" to produce a product that the causes "IRS wage sales tax" and "Company sales tax" to snowball in the market place.

Only Companies make money on products and services in the market place; therefore, all the products and services in the market will be tainted with the "IRS wage sales tax," "IRS snowball wage sales tax," "Company sales tax," and "Company snowball sales tax." Any purchase made in the market place must pay the "IRS wage sales tax," "IRS snow- ball wage sales tax," "Company sales tax," and "Company snowball sales tax."

When making purchases in the market place, a "gross wage earner" who shelled out his "IRS wage tax" to the Federal government pays also the "IRS wage sales tax," "IRS snowball wage sales tax," "Company sales tax" and "Company snowball sales tax." The "gross wage earner"

pays "IRS wage tax" three times over and the "Company tax" two times over.

A non-wage earner is only exposed to the "IRS wage sales tax," "IRS snowball wage sales tax," "Company sales tax" and "Company snowball sales tax." The non-wage earner pays both the "IRS wage tax" and Company tax two times over.

The Federal government collects the "gross wage earners" "IRS wage tax" and takes a table percentage of the "IRS wage sales tax," "IRS snowball wage sales tax," "Company sales tax" and "Company snowball sales tax."

The Federal government sales tax collections get hid- den in the Treasury.

COMPANY AND SOCIAL SECURITY SALES TAX
(16th Amendment Multi tax)

A Company sends the "Company tax" and "Social Security wage tax" to the Federal government as prescribed under the 16th Amendment.

The Company transfers "Company tax" and "Social Security wage tax" to the market place as sale taxes.

"Other Companies" sends their "Company tax" and "Social Security wage tax" to the Federal government. Companies use "other Companies" to produce a product that causes "Social Security wage sales tax" and "Company sales tax" to snowball in the market place.

Only Companies make money on products and services in the market place; therefore, all the products and services in the market will be tainted with the "Social Security wage sales tax," "Social Security snowball wage sales tax," "Company sales tax," and "Company snowball sales tax." Any purchase made in the market place must pay the "Social Security wage sales tax," "Social Security snow-

ball wage sales tax," "Company sales tax," and "Company snowball sales tax."

When making purchases in the market place, a "gross wage earner" who shelled out his "Social Security wage tax" to the Federal government pays also the "Social Security wage sales tax," "Social

Security snowball wage sales tax," "Company sales tax" and "Company snowball sales tax." The "gross wage earner" pays "Social Security wage tax" three times over and the "Company tax" two times over.

A non-wage earner is only exposed to the "Social Security wage sales tax," "Social Security snowball wage sales tax," "Company sales tax" and "Company snowball sales tax."

The non-wage earner pays both the "Social Security wage tax" and Company tax two times over.

The Federal government collects the "gross wage earners" "Social Security wage tax" and takes a table percentage of the "Social Security wage sales tax," "Social Security snowball wage sales tax," "Company sales tax" and "Company snowball sales tax."

The Federal government sales tax collections get hid- den in the Treasury.

COMPANY AND MEDICARE SALES TAX
(16th Amendment Multi tax)

A Company sends the "Company tax" and "Medicare wage tax" to the Federal government as prescribed under the 16th Amendment.

The Company transfers "Company tax" and "Medicare wage tax" to the market place as sale taxes.

"Other Companies" sends their "Company tax" and "Medicare wage tax" to the Federal government. Companies use "other Companies" to produce a product that the causes "Medicare wage sales tax" and "Company sales tax" to snowball in the market place.

Only Companies make money on products and services in the market place; therefore, all the products and services in the market will be tainted with the "Medicare wage sales tax," "Medicare snowball wage sales tax," "Company sales tax," and "Company snowball sales tax." Any purchase made in the market place must pay the "Medicare wage sales tax," "Medicare snowball wage sales tax," "Company sales tax," and "Company snowball sales tax."

When making purchases in the market place, a "gross wage earner" who shelled out his "Medicare wage tax" to the Federal government pays also the "Medicare wage sales tax," "Medicare snowball wage sales tax," "Company sales tax" and "Company snowball sales tax." The "gross wage earner" pays "Medicare wage tax" three times over and the "Company tax" two times over. A non-wage earner is only exposed to the "Medicare wage sales tax," "Medicare snowball wage sales tax," "Company sales tax" and "Company snowball sales tax." The non-wage earner pays both the "Medicare wage tax" and Company tax two times over.

The Federal government collects the Company tax, "gross wage earners" "Medicare wage tax" and takes a table percentage of the "Medicare wage sales tax," "Medicare snowball wage sales tax," "Company sales tax" and "Company snowball sales tax."

The Federal government sales tax collections get hid- den in the Treasury.

COMPANY AND UNEMPLOYMENT SALES TAX
(16th Amendment Multi tax)

A Company sends the "Company tax" and "Unemployment wage tax" to the Federal government as prescribed under the 16th Amendment.

The Company transfers "Company tax" and "Unemployment wage tax" to the market place as sale taxes. "Other Companies" sends their "Company tax" and "Unemployment wage tax" to the Federal government. Companies use "other Companies" to produce a product that the causes "Unemployment wage sales tax" and "Company

sales tax" to snowball in the market place.

Only Companies make money on products and services in the market place; therefore, all the products and services in the market will be tainted with the "Unemployment wage sales tax," "Unemployment snowball wage sales tax," "Company sales tax," and "Company snowball sales tax." Any purchase made in the market place must pay the "Unemployment wage sales tax," "Unemployment snow- ball wage sales tax," "Company sales tax," and "Company snowball sales tax."

When making purchases in the market place, a "gross wage earner" who shelled out his "Unemployment wage tax" to the Federal government pays also the "Unemployment wage sales tax," "Unemployment snowball wage sales tax," "Company sales tax" and "Company snowball sales tax." The "gross wage earner" pays "Unemployment wage tax" three times over and the "Company tax" two times over.

Anon-wage earner is only exposed to the "Unemployment wage sales tax," "Unemployment snowball wage sales tax," "Company sales tax" and "Company snowball sales tax." The non-wage earner pays both the "Unemployment wage tax" and Company tax two times over.

The Federal government collects the "gross wage earners" "Unemployment wage tax" and takes a table percent- age of the "Unemployment wage sales tax," "Unemployment snowball wage sales tax," "Company sales tax" and "Company snowball sales tax."

The Federal government sales tax collections get hid- den in the Treasury.

DEMISE MIDDLE CLASS COMPANY OWNER!

DEMISE MIDDLE CLASS COMPANY TAX

The Company had to pay the following taxes to Federal government:

- Company tax

In order to preserve the Company's profit, the Company transmits the following Company tax as sales' taxes to the market place:

- Company sales tax

The Company has to rely on "other company" for support.

The "other company" pays the following taxes to Federal government:

- Other company tax

In order to preserve a profit, all these "other company" transmits the following "Other company tax" as a sales tax to the market place:

- Other company sales tax the following develops:
- Other company sale tax becomes "snowball company sale tax"

The "snowball" tax is added in the following Federal government's transmitted sales taxes:

- Company sale tax
- Snowball company sales tax

The following are added to the company's product or service:

- Company's sales tax
- Snowball company sales tax

The middle-class company is forced to compete with other companies in order to sell enough of its product or service to produce a profit.

The United State Treasury contains the following hid- den sales tax:

- Company's sales tax
- Snowball company sales tax

DEMISE MIDDLE CLASS EMPLOYEE
WAGE TAX

The Company had to pay the following taxes to Federal government:

- Company tax

In order to preserve the Company's profit, the Company transmits the following Company tax as sales' taxes to the market place:

- Company sales tax

The Company has to rely on "other company" for support.

The "other company" pays the following taxes to Federal government:

- Other company tax

In order to preserve a profit, all these "other company" transmits the following "Other company tax as a sales tax to the market place:

- Other company sales tax the following develops:
- Other company sale tax becomes "snowball company sale tax"

The "snowball" tax is added in the following Federal government's transmitted sales taxes:

- Company sale tax
- Snowball company sales tax

The following are added to the company's product or service:

- Company's sales tax
- Snowball company sales tax

The middle-class company is forced to compete with other companies in order to sell enough of its product or service to produce a profit.

The United State Treasury contains the following hid- den sales tax:

- Company's sales tax
- Snowball company sales tax

DEMISE MIDDLE CLASS COMPANY TAX WAGE TAX WITH ENTITLEMENTS

The Company had to pay the following taxes to Federal government:

- Company tax
- Company wage tax
- Company social security wage tax
- Company Medicare wage tax
- Company unemployment wage tax

In order to preserve the Company, profit the Company transmits the following taxes as sales' taxes to the market place:

- Company sale tax
- Company wage sales tax
- Company social security wage sales tax
- Company Medicare wage sales tax
- Company unemployment wage sales tax

The Company has to rely on "other company" for support.

The "other company" pays the following taxes to Federal government:

- Other company tax
- Other company wage tax
- Other company social security wage tax
- Other company Medicare wage tax

- Other company unemployment wage tax

In order to preserve a profit, the company" transmits the following taxes as sales' taxes to the market place:

- Other company sales tax
- Other company wage sales tax
- Other company social security wage sales tax
- Other company Medicare wage sales tax
- Other company unemployment wage sales tax the following develops:
- Other company sales tax becomes "snowball company sales tax"
- Other company wage sales tax" becomes "snowball wage sales tax"
- Other company social security wage sales tax becomes "snowball social security wage sales tax"
- Other company Medicare wage sales tax becomes "snowball Medicare wage sales tax"
- Other company unemployment wage sales tax becomes snowball unemployment wage sales tax"

The snowballs" are added in the following to the Federal government's transmitted sales taxes:

- Company sale tax
- Company wage sales tax
- Company social security wage sales tax

- Company Medicare wage sales tax
- Company unemployment wage sales tax
- Snowball company sales tax
- Snowball wage sales tax
- Snowball social security wage sales tax
- Snowball Medicare wage sales tax
- Snowball unemployment wage sales tax

The following are added to the Company product or service:

- Company sale tax
- Company wage sales tax
- Company social security wage sales tax
- Company Medicare wage sales tax
- Company unemployment wage sales tax
- Snowball wage sales tax
- Snowball social security wage sales tax
- Snowball Medicare wage sales tax
- Snowball unemployment wage sales tax

The middle-class company is forced to compete with other companies in order to sell enough of its product or service to produce a profit.

The United State Treasury contains the following hid- den sales tax:

- Company sale tax
- Company wage sales tax
- Company social security wage sales tax
- Company Medicare wage sales tax
- Company unemployment wage sales tax
- Snowball wage sales tax
- Snowball social security wage sales tax
- Snowball Medicare wage sales tax
- Snowball unemployment wage sales tax

DEMISE MIDDLE CLASS COMPANY TAX WAGE TAX WITH ENTITLEMENTS

HEALTHCARE INCREASE MINIMUM WAGE AND COMPANY TAX

The Company had to pay the following taxes to Federal government:

- Company tax
- Company wage tax
- Company social security wage tax
- Company Medicare wage tax
- Company unemployment wage tax
- Company healthcare wage tax
- Company increases minimum wage tax

In order to preserve the Company, profit the Company transmits the following taxes as sales' taxes to the market place:

- Company sales tax
- Company wage sales tax
- Company social security wage sales tax
- Company Medicare wage sales tax
- Company unemployment wage sales tax
- Company healthcare wage sales tax
- Company increases minimum wage sales tax

The Company has to rely on other company for support.

The other company pays the following taxes to Federal government:

- Other company tax
- Other company wage tax
- Other company social security wage tax
- Other company Medicare wage tax
- Other company unemployment wage tax
- Other Company healthcare wage tax
- Other Company increase minimum wage tax

In order to preserve a profit, all these other company transmits the following taxes as sales' taxes to the market place:

- Other company sales tax
- Other company wage sales tax
- Other company social security wage sales tax
- Other company Medicare wage sales tax
- Other company unemployment wage sales tax
- Other Company healthcare wage sales tax
- Other Company increase minimum wage sales tax The following develops:

- Other company sales tax becomes snowball company sales tax
- Other company wage sales tax becomes snowball wage sales tax
- Other company social security wage sales tax becomes snowball social security wage sales tax

- Other company Medicare wage sales tax becomes snowball Medicare wage sales tax
- Other company unemployment wage sales tax becomes snowball unemployment wage sales tax
- Other company healthcare wage sales tax becomes snowball healthcare wage sales tax
- Other Company increase minimum wage sales tax becomes snowball increase minimum wage sales tax

The snowballs are added in the following to the Federal government's transmitted sales taxes:

- Company sales tax
- Company wage sales tax
- Company social security wage sales tax
- Company Medicare wage sales tax
- Company unemployment wage sales tax
- Company healthcare wage sales tax
- Company increases minimum wage sales tax
- Snowball company sales tax
- Snowball wage sales tax
- Snowball social security wage sales tax
- Snowball Medicare wage sales tax
- Snowball unemployment wage sales tax
- Snowball healthcare wage sales tax

- snowball increase minimum wage sales tax

The following are added to the Company product or service:

- Company sales tax
- Company wage sales tax
- Company social security wage sales tax
- Company Medicare wage sales tax
- Company unemployment wage sales tax
- Company healthcare wage sales tax
- Company increases minimum wage sales tax
- Snowball company sales tax
- Snowball wage sales tax
- Snowball social security wage sales tax
- Snowball Medicare wage sales tax
- Snowball unemployment wage sales tax
- Snowball healthcare wage sales tax
- Snowball increases minimum wage sales tax

The middle-class company is forced to compete with other companies in order to sell enough of its product or service to produce a profit

The United State Treasury contains the following hid- den sales tax:

- Company sales tax
- Company wage sales tax

- Company social security wage sales tax
- Company Medicare wage sales tax
- Company unemployment wage sales tax
- Snowball company sales tax
- Company healthcare wage sales tax
- Company increases minimum wage sales tax
- Snowball wage sales tax
- Snowball social security wage sales tax
- Snowball Medicare wage sales tax
- Snowball unemployment wage sales tax
- Snowball healthcare wage sales tax
- snowball increase minimum wage sales tax

FEDERAL TAX COLLECTION WITH ENTITLEMENTS HEALTHCARE INCREASE MINIMUM WAGE AND COMPANY TAX

The Company pays the following taxes to Federal government:

- Company tax
- Company wage tax
- Company social security wage tax
- Company Medicare wage tax
- Company unemployment wage tax
- Company healthcare wage tax
- Company increases minimum wage tax

In order to preserve the Company, profit the Company transmits the following taxes as sales' taxes to the market place:

- Company sales tax
- Company wage sales tax
- Company social security wage sales tax
- Company Medicare wage sales tax
- Company unemployment wage sales tax
- Company healthcare wage sales tax
- Company increases minimum wage sales tax

The Company has to rely on other company for support.

The other company pays the following taxes to Federal government:

- Other company tax
- Other company wage tax
- Other company social security wage tax
- Other company Medicare wage tax
- Other company unemployment wage tax
- Other Company healthcare wage tax
- Other Company increase minimum wage tax

In order to preserve a profit, all these other company transmits the following taxes as sales' taxes to the market place:

- Other company sales tax
- Other company wage sales tax
- Other company social security wage sales tax
- Other company Medicare wage sales tax
- Other company unemployment wage sales tax
- Other Company healthcare wage sales tax
- Other Company increase minimum wage sales tax The following develops:
- Other company sales tax becomes snowball company sales tax
- Other company wage sales tax becomes snowball wage sales tax
- Other company social security wage sales tax becomes snowball social security wage sales tax

- Other company Medicare wage sales tax becomes snowball Medicare wage sales tax
- Other company unemployment wage sales tax becomes snowball unemployment wage sales tax
- Other company healthcare wage sales tax becomes snowball healthcare wage sales tax
- Other Company increase minimum wage sales tax becomes snowball increase minimum wage sales tax

The snowballs are added in the following to the Federal government's transmitted sales taxes:

- Company sales tax
- Company wage sales tax
- Company social security wage sales tax
- Company Medicare wage sales tax
- Company unemployment wage sales tax
- Company healthcare wage sales tax
- Company increases minimum wage sales tax
- Snowball company sales tax
- Snowball wage sales tax
- Snowball social security wage sales tax
- Snowball Medicare wage sales tax
- Snowball unemployment wage sales tax
- Snowball healthcare wage sales tax
- Snowball increases minimum wage sales tax Total tax

Company sales tax

- Company wage sales tax
- Company social security wage sales tax
- Company Medicare wage sales tax
- Company unemployment wage sales tax
- Company increases minimum wage sales tax Total snowball tax = tax
- Snowball company sales tax
- Snowball wage sales tax
- Snowball social security wage sales tax
- Snowball Medicare wage sales tax
- Snowball unemployment wage sales tax
- Snowball healthcare wage sales tax
- Snowball Company increases minimum wage sales
- Snowball increases minimum wage sales tax

Gross company income = (Company expenses + Profit+ Total tax + Total snowball tax)

New Company Tax = Tax% x Gross company income Tax% is taken from a table.

The Federal collection=Tax% x (Company expenses+ Profit+ Total tax + Total snowball tax)

“Reserved Power Clause”

Popularity Vote

(Governor, County Executive, City Mayor, Town Mayor, Village Mayor, State Jude, Senator, President)

Constitution

Bill of Rights

10th Amendment

Delegated Clause (Constant)
Reserved Power Clause (Popularity Vote State Governor)

POPULARITY VOTE

State Governor

The 10th Amendment states "the powers (State) not delegated to the United States by the Constitution, nor prohibited by it (Constitution) to the States (legislature), are reserved (reserved power clause) to the States (legislature) respectively, or to the State people (quasi equal populated districts)."

In other words, "the powers (State) not delegated to the United States by the Constitution, or not prohibited (not allowed) by it (Constitution) to the States (legislature), are reserved (reserved power clause) to the States (legislature) respectively, or to the State people (quasi equal populated districts)."

In other words, "the powers (State) not delegated to the United States by the Constitution, or not allowed by it (Constitution) to the States (legislature), are reserved (reserved power clause) to the

States (legislature) respectively, or to the State people (quasi equal populated districts)."

In other words, "the powers (State) not delegated to the United States by the Constitution, or allowed by it (Constitution) to the States (legislature), are reserved (reserved power clause) to the States (legislature) respectively, or to the State people (quasi equal populated districts)." The "reserved power clause" applies to the States legislature (quasi equal populated districts) or to the State people (quasi equal populated districts).

The "reserved power clause" may be applied in the following two ways to measure the popularity of the Governor: Through the State legislature members "pros and cons" voting. Through the State people voting within "quasi equal populated districts" counting the "pros and cons" of the "quasi equal populated districts"

COMPUTERS MEASURE POPULARITY GOVERNOR

While a Person is balloting in a voting booth, a computer may be used to automatically measure the popularity of the Governor. A referendum at election time may be displayed to question the approval or disapproval of the Governor. As the person makes a choice in a States polling booth, the computer immediately registers the "pros and cons" responses. At the end of the day, the computer "pros and cons" responses results are automatically published in the State.

The total responses signify the popularity of the Governor.

Through using a spread sheet flow chart, a computer may be programmed.

Based upon the counting of “pros and cons” “quasi equal populated districts,” “Mob Rule” is eliminated.

“Popularity voting” will jog the governor’s memory knowing that the States legislature and people within “quasi equal popularity districts have the power to impeach him.

Constitution

Bill of Rights

10th Amendment

Delegated Clause (Constant)

Reserved Power Clause (Popularity Vote County Executive)

POPULARITY VOTE

County Executive

The 10th Amendment states "the powers (County) not delegated to the United States by the Constitution, nor prohibited by it (Constitution) to the Counties (legislature), are reserved (reserved power clause) to the Counties (legislature) respectively, or to the County people (quasi equal populated districts)."

In other words, "the powers (County) not delegated to the United States by the Constitution, or not prohibited (not allowed) by it (Constitution) to the Counties (legislature), are reserved (reserved power clause) to the Counties (legislature) respectively, or to the County people (quasi equal populated districts)."

In other words, "the powers (County) not delegated to the United States by the Constitution, or not allowed by it (Constitution) to the Counties (legislature), are reserved (reserved power clause) to

the Counties (legislature) respectively, or to the County people (quasi equal populated districts)."

In other words, "the powers (County) not delegated to the United States by the Constitution, or allowed by it (Constitution) to the Counties (legislature), are reserved (reserved power clause) to the Counties (legislature) respectively, or to the County people (quasi equal populated districts)."

The "reserved power clause" applies to the County legislature (quasi equal populated districts) or to the County people (quasi equal populated districts).

The "reserved power clause" may be applied in the following two ways to measure the popularity of the County executive:

Through the County legislature members "pros and cons" voting

Through the County people voting within "quasi equal populated districts" counting the "pros and cons" of the "quasi equal populated districts"

COMPUTERS MEASURE POPULARITY COUNTY EXECUTIVE

While a Person is balloting in a voting booth, a computer may be used to automatically measure the popularity of the County executive. A referendum at election time may be displayed to question the approval or disapproval of the County executive. As the person makes a choice in a States polling booth, the computer immediately registers the "pros and cons" responses.

At the end of the day, the computer "pros and cons" responses results are automatically published in the County. The total responses signify the popularity of the County executive. Through using a spread sheet flow chart, a computer may be programmed.

Based upon the counting of "pros and cons" "quasi equal populated districts," "Mob Rule" is eliminated.

"Popularity voting" will jog the County executive's memory knowing that the County legislature and people within "quasi equal popularity districts have the power to impeach him.

Constitution

Bill of Rights

10th Amendment

Delegated Clause (Constant)

Reserved Power Clause (Popularity Vote City Mayor)

POPULARITY VOTE

City Mayor

The 10th Amendment states "the powers (City) not delegated to the United States by the Constitution, nor prohibited by it (Constitution) to the Cities (council), are reserved (reserved power clause) to the Cities (council) respectively, or to the city people (quasi equal populated districts)."

In other words, "the powers (City) not delegated to the United States by the Constitution, or not prohibited (not allowed) by it (Constitution) to the Cities (council), are reserved (reserved power clause) to the Cities (council) respectively, or to the city people (quasi equal populated districts)."

In other words, "the powers (City) not delegated to the United States by the Constitution, or not allowed by it (Constitution) to the Cities (council), are reserved (reserved power clause) to the

Cities (council) respectively, or to the city people (quasi equal populated districts)."

In other words, "the powers (City) not delegated to the United States by the Constitution, or allowed by it (Constitution) to the Cities (council), are reserved (reserved power clause) to the Cities (council) respectively, or to the city people (quasi equal populated districts)."

The "reserved power clause" applies to the city council (quasi equal populated districts) or to the city people (quasi equal populated districts).

The "reserved power clause" may be applied in the following two ways to measure the popularity of the city mayor: Through the City council members "pros and cons" voting. Through the City people voting within "quasi equal populated districts" counting the "pros and cons" of the "quasi equal populated districts"

COMPUTERS MEASURE POPULARITY

CITY MAYOR

While a Person is balloting in a voting booth, a computer may be used to automatically measure the popularity of the city mayor. A referendum at election time may be displayed to question the approval or disapproval of the City mayor. As the person makes a choice in a polling booth, the computer immediately registers the "pros and cons" responses.

At the end of the day, the computer "pros and cons" responses results are automatically published in the city. The total responses signify the popularity of the city mayor.

Through using a spread sheet flow chart, a computer may be programmed.

Based upon the counting of "pros and cons" "quasi equal populated districts," "Mob Rule" is eliminated.

"Popularity voting" will jog the city mayor's memory knowing that the city legislature and people within "quasi equal popularity districts have the power to impeach him.

Constitution

Bill of Rights

10th Amendment

Delegated Clause (Constant)

Reserved Power Clause (Popularity Vote Town Mayor)

POPULARITY VOTE

Town Mayor

The 10th Amendment states "the powers (Town) not delegated to the United States by the Constitution, nor prohibited by it (Constitution) to the Towns (council), are reserved (reserved power clause) to the Towns (council) respectively, or to the Town people (quasi equal populated districts)."

In other words, "the powers (Town) not delegated to the United States by the Constitution, or not prohibited (not allowed) by it (Constitution) to the Towns (council), are reserved (reserved power clause) to the Towns (council) respectively, or to the Town people (quasi equal populated districts)."

In other words, "the powers (Town) not delegated to the United States by the Constitution, or not allowed by it (Constitution) to the Towns (council), are reserved (reserved power clause) to the

Towns (council) respectively, or to the Town people (quasi equal populated districts)."

In other words, "the powers (Town) not delegated to the United States by the Constitution, or allowed by it (Constitution) to the Towns (council), are reserved (reserved power clause) to the Towns (council) respectively, or to the Town people (quasi equal populated districts)."

The "reserved power clause" applies to the Town council (quasi equal populated districts) or to the Town people (quasi equal populated districts).

The "reserved power clause" may be applied in the following two ways to measure the popularity of the Town mayor:

Through the Town council members "pros and cons" voting

Through the Town people voting within "quasi equal populated districts" counting the "pros and cons" of the "quasi equal populated districts"

COMPUTERS MEASURE POPULARITY TOWN MAYOR

While a Person is balloting in a voting booth, a computer may be used to automatically measure the popularity of the Town mayor. A referendum at election time may be displayed to question the approval or disapproval of the Town mayor. As the person makes a choice in a polling booth, the computer immediately registers the "pros and cons" responses. At the end of the day, the computer "pros and cons" responses results are automatically published in the Town. The total responses signify the popularity of the Town mayor.

Through using a spread sheet flow chart, a computer may be programmed.

Based upon the counting of "pros and cons" "quasi equal populated districts," "Mob Rule" is eliminated.

"Popularity voting" will jog the Town mayor's memory knowing that the Town legislature and people within "quasi equal popularity districts have the power to impeach him.

Constitution

Bill of Rights

10th Amendment

Delegated Clause (Constant)

Reserved Power Clause (Popularity Vote Village Mayor)

POPULARITY VOTE

Village Mayor

The 10th Amendment states "the powers (Village) not delegated to the United States by the Constitution, nor prohibited by it (Constitution) to the Villages (council), are reserved (reserved power clause) to the Villages (council) respectively, or to the Village people (quasi equal populated districts)."

In other words, "the powers (Village) not delegated to the United States by the Constitution, or not prohibited (not allowed) by it (Constitution) to the Villages (council), are reserved (reserved power clause) to the Villages (council) respectively, or to the Village people (quasi equal populated districts)."

In other words, "the powers (Village) not delegated to the United States by the Constitution, or not allowed by it (Constitution) to the Villages (council), are reserved (reserved power clause) to the

Villages (council) respectively, or to the Village people (quasi equal populated districts)."

In other words, "the powers (Village) not delegated to the United States by the Constitution, or allowed by it (Constitution) to the Villages (council), are reserved (reserved power clause) to the Villages (council) respectively, or to the Village people (quasi equal populated districts)."

The "reserved power clause" applies to the Village council (quasi equal populated districts) or to the Village people (quasi equal populated districts).

The "reserved power clause" may be applied in the following two ways to measure the popularity of the Village mayor:

Through the Village council members "pros and cons" voting

Through the Village people voting within "quasi equal populated districts" counting the "pros and cons" of the "quasi equal populated districts"

COMPUTERS MEASURE POPULARITY VILLAGE MAYOR

While a Person is balloting in a voting booth, a computer may be used to automatically measure the popularity of the Village mayor. A referendum at election time may be displayed to question the approval or disapproval of the Village mayor. As the person makes a choice in a States polling booth, the computer immediately registers the "pros and cons" responses.

At the end of the day, the computer "pros and cons" responses results are automatically published in the Village. The total responses signify the popularity of the Village mayor.

Through using a spread sheet flow chart, a computer may be programmed.

Based upon the counting of "pros and cons" "quasi equal populated districts," "Mob Rule" is eliminated.

"Popularity voting" will jog the Village mayor's memory knowing that the Village legislature and people within "quasi equal popularity districts have the power to impeach him.

Constitution

Bill of Rights

10th Amendment

Delegated Clause (Constant)

Reserved Power Clause (Popularity Vote Stage Judge)

POPULARITY VOTE

Stage Judge

The 10th Amendment states "the powers (State) not delegated to the United States by the Constitution, nor prohibited by it (Constitution) to the States (legislature), are reserved (reserved power clause) to the States (legislature) respectively, or to the State people (quasi equal populated districts)."

In other words, "the powers (State) not delegated to the United States by the Constitution, or not prohibited (not allowed) by it (Constitution) to the States (legislature), are reserved (reserved power clause) to the States (legislature) respectively, or to the State people (quasi equal populated districts)."

In other words, "the powers (State) not delegated to the United States by the Constitution, or not allowed by it (Constitution) to the States (legislature), are reserved (reserved power clause) to the

States (legislature) respectively, or to the State people (quasi equal populated districts)."

In other words, "the powers (State) not delegated to the United States by the Constitution, or allowed by it (Constitution) to the States (legislature), are reserved (reserved power clause) to the States (legislature) respectively, or to the State people (quasi equal populated districts)." The "reserved power clause" applies to the State legislature (quasi equal populated districts) or to the State people (quasi equal populated districts).

The "reserved power clause" may be applied in the following two ways to measure the popularity of the State judge:

Through the State legislature members "pros and cons" voting

Through the State people voting within "quasi equal populated districts" counting the "pros and cons" of the "quasi equal populated districts"

COMPUTERS MEASURE POPULARITY STATE JUDGE

While a Person is balloting in a voting booth, a computer may be used to automatically measure the popularity of the State judge. A referendum at election time may be displayed to question the approval or disapproval of the State judge. As the person makes a choice in a States polling booth, the computer immediately registers the "pros and cons" responses.

At the end of the day, the computer "pros and cons" responses results are automatically published in the State. The total responses signify the popularity of the State judge.

Through using a spread sheet flow chart, a computer may be programmed.

Based upon the counting of "pros and cons" "quasi equal populated districts," "Mob Rule" is eliminated.

Popularity voting will jog the State judge's memory knowing that the State legislature and people within "quasi equal popularity districts have the power to impeach him.

Constitution

Bill of Rights

10th Amendment

Delegated Clause (Constant)
Reserved Power Clause (Popularity Vote US Senator)

POPULARITY VOTE
United States Senator

The 10th Amendment states "the powers (State) not delegated to the United States by the Constitution, nor prohibited by it (Constitution) to the States (legislature), are reserved (reserved power clause) to the States (legislature) respectively, or to the State people (quasi equal populated districts)."

In other words, "the powers (State) not delegated to the United States by the Constitution, or not prohibited (not allowed) by it (Constitution) to the States (legislature), are reserved (reserved power clause) to the States (legislature) respectively, or to the State people (quasi equal populated districts)."

In other words, "the powers (State) not delegated to the United States by the Constitution, or not allowed by it (Constitution) to the States (legislature), are reserved (reserved power clause) to the

States (legislature) respectively, or to the State people (quasi equal populated districts)."

In other words, "the powers (State) not delegated to the United States by the Constitution, or allowed by it (Constitution) to the States (legislature), are reserved (reserved power clause) to the States (legislature) respectively, or to the State people (quasi equal populated districts)." The "reserved power clause" applies to the State legislature (quasi equal populated districts) or to the State people (quasi equal populated districts).

The "reserved power clause" may be applied in the following two ways to measure the popularity of the United States senator:

Through the State legislature members "pros and cons" voting. Through the State people voting within "quasi equal populated districts" counting the "pros and cons" of the "quasi equal populated districts"

COMPUTERS MEASURE POPULARITY UNITED STATES SENATOR

While a Person is balloting in a voting booth, a computer may be used to automatically measure the popularity of the United States senator. A referendum at election time may be displayed to question the approval or disapproval of the United States senator. As the person makes a choice in a polling booth, the computer immediately registers the "pros and cons" responses.

At the end of the day, the computer "pros and cons" responses results are automatically published in the State. The total responses signify the popularity of the United States senator.

Through using a spread sheet flow chart, a computer may be programmed.

Based upon the counting of "pros and cons" "quasi equal populated districts," "Mob Rule" is eliminated.

"Popularity voting" will jog the United States senator's memory knowing that the State legislature and people within "quasi equal popularity districts have the power to impeach him.

Constitution

Bill of Rights

10th Amendment

Delegated Clause (Constant)

Reserved Power Clause (Popularity Vote US President)

POPULARITY VOTE

United States President

The 10th Amendment states "the powers (State) not delegated to the United States by the Constitution, nor prohibited by it (Constitution) to the States (legislature), are reserved (reserved power clause) to the States (legislature) respectively, or to the State people (quasi equal populated districts)."

In other words, "the powers (State) not delegated to the United States by the Constitution, or not prohibited (not allowed) by it (Constitution) to the States (legislature), are reserved (reserved power clause) to the States (legislature) respectively, or to the State people (quasi equal populated districts)."

In other words, "the powers (State) not delegated to the United States by the Constitution, or not allowed by it (Constitution) to the States (legislature), are reserved (reserved power clause) to the States (legislature) respectively, or to the State people (quasi equal populated districts)."

In other words, "the powers (State) not delegated to the United States by the Constitution, or allowed by it (Constitution) to the States (legislature), are reserved (reserved power clause) to the States (legislature) respectively, or to the State people (quasi equal populated districts)." The "reserved power clause" applies to the State legislature (quasi equal populated districts) or to the State people (quasi equal populated districts). The "reserved

power clause" may be applied in the following two ways to measure the popularity of the United States President:

Through the State legislature members "pros and cons" voting. Through the State people voting within "quasi equal populated districts" counting the "pros and cons" of the "quasi equal populated districts"

COMPUTERS MEASURE POPULARITY UNITED STATES PRESIDENT

While a Person is balloting in a voting booth, a computer may be used to automatically measure the popularity of the United States President. A referendum at election time may be displayed to question the approval or disapproval of the United States President. As the person makes a choice in a States polling booth, the computer immediately registers the "pros and cons" responses.

At the end of the day, the computer "pros and cons" responses results are automatically published in the State. The total responses signify the popularity of the United States President.

Through using a spread sheet flow chart, a computer may be programmed.

Based upon the counting of "pros and cons" "quasi equal populated districts," "Mob Rule" is eliminated.

"Popularity voting" will jog the United States President's memory knowing that the State legislature and people within "quasi equal popularity districts have the power to impeach him.

"Reserved Power Clause"

Popularity Wage Tax

(IRS, Social Security, Medicare, Unemployment)

Constitution

Bill of Rights

10th Amendment

Delegated Clause (Constant)
Reserved Power Clause (Popularity Vote IRS Tax)

POPULARITY VOTE
IRS Tax

The 10th Amendment states "the powers (State) not delegated to the United States by the Constitution, nor prohibited by it (Constitution) to the States (legislature), are reserved (reserved power clause) to the States (legislature) respectively, or to the State people (quasi equal populated districts)."

In other words, "the powers (State) not delegated to the United States by the Constitution, or not prohibited (not allowed) by it (Constitution) to the States (legislature), are reserved (reserved power clause) to the States (legislature) respectively, or to the State people (quasi equal populated districts)."

In other words, "the powers (State) not delegated to the United States by the Constitution, or not allowed by it (Constitution) to the States (legislature), are reserved (reserved power clause) to the

States (legislature) respectively, or to the State people (quasi equal populated districts)."

In other words, "the powers (State) not delegated to the United States by the Constitution, or allowed by it (Constitution) to the States (legislature), are reserved (reserved power clause) to the States (legislature) respectively, or to the State people (quasi equal populated districts)." The "reserved power clause" applies to the States legislature (quasi equal populated districts) or to the State people (quasi equal populated districts).

The "reserved power clause" may be applied in the following two ways to measure the popularity of the IRS tax:

Through the State legislature members "pros and cons" voting. Through the State people voting within "quasi equal populated districts" counting the "pros and cons" of the "quasi equal populated districts"

COMPUTERS MEASURE POPULARITY IRS TAX

While a Person is balloting in a voting booth, a computer may be used to automatically measure the popularity of the IRS tax. A referendum at election time may be displayed to question the approval or disapproval of the IRS tax. As the person makes a choice in a States polling booth, the computer immediately registers the "pros and cons" responses. At the end of the day, the computer "pros and cons" responses results are automatically published in the State.

The total responses signify the popularity of the IRS tax.

Through using a spread sheet flow chart, a computer may be programmed.

Based upon the counting of "pros and cons" "quasi equal populated districts," "Mob Rule" is eliminated.

Popularity voting the IRS tax will indicate to the States legislature and people within "quasi equal popularity districts" to repeal the IRS tax.

Constitution

Bill of Rights

10th Amendment

Delegated Clause (Constant)

Reserved Power Clause (Popularity Vote Social Security Tax)

POPULARITY VOTE

Social Security Wage Tax

The 10th Amendment states "the powers (State) not delegated to the United States by the Constitution, nor prohibited by it (Constitution) to the States (legislature), are reserved (reserved power clause) to the States (legislature) respectively, or to the State people (quasi equal populated districts)."

In other words, "the powers (State) not delegated to the United States by the Constitution, or not prohibited (not allowed) by it (Constitution) to the States (legislature), are reserved (reserved power clause) to the States (legislature) respectively, or to the State people (quasi equal populated districts)."

In other words, "the powers (State) not delegated to the United States by the Constitution, or not allowed by it (Constitution) to the States (legislature), are reserved (reserved power clause) to the

States (legislature) respectively, or to the State people (quasi equal populated districts)."

In other words, "the powers (State) not delegated to the United States by the Constitution, or allowed by it (Constitution) to the States (legislature), are reserved (reserved power clause) to the States (legislature) respectively, or to the State people (quasi equal populated districts)." The "reserved power clause" applies to the States legislature (quasi equal populated districts) or to the State people (quasi equal populated districts). The "reserved power clause" may be applied in the following two ways to measure the popularity of the Social Security wage tax:

Through the State legislature members "pros and cons" voting. Through the State people voting within "quasi equal populated districts" counting the "pros and cons" of the "quasi equal populated districts"

COMPUTERS MEASURE POPULARITY SOCIAL SECURITY WAGE TAX

While a Person is balloting in a voting booth, a computer may be used to automatically measure the popularity of the Social Security wage tax. A referendum at election time may be displayed to question the approval or disapproval of the Social Security wage tax. As the person makes a choice in a States polling booth, the computer immediately registers the "pros and cons" responses. At the end of the day, the computer "pros and cons" responses results are automatically published in the State. The total responses signify the popularity of the Social Security wage tax. Through using a spread sheet flow chart, a computer may be programmed.

Based upon the counting of "pros and cons" "quasi equal populated districts," "Mob Rule" is eliminated.

"Popularity voting" the Social Security wage tax will indicate to the States legislature and people within "quasi equal popularity districts" to repeal the Social Security wage tax.

Constitution

Bill of Rights

10th Amendment

Delegated Clause (Constant)

Reserved Power Clause (Popularity Vote Medicare Tax)

POPULARITY VOTE

Medicare Wage Tax

The 10th Amendment states "the powers (State) not delegated to the United States by the Constitution, nor prohibited by it (Constitution) to the States (legislature), are reserved (reserved power clause) to the States (legislature) respectively, or to the State people (quasi equal populated districts)."

In other words, "the powers (State) not delegated to the United States by the Constitution, or not prohibited (not allowed) by it (Constitution) to the States (legislature), are reserved (reserved power clause) to the States (legislature) respectively, or to the State people (quasi equal populated districts)."

In other words, "the powers (State) not delegated to the United States by the Constitution, or not allowed by it (Constitution) to the States (legislature), are reserved (reserved power clause) to the

States (legislature) respectively, or to the State people (quasi equal populated districts)."

In other words, "the powers (State) not delegated to the United States by the Constitution, or allowed by it (Constitution) to the States (legislature), are reserved (reserved power clause) to the States (legislature) respectively, or to the State people (quasi equal populated districts)." The "reserved power clause" applies to the States legislature (quasi equal populated districts) or to the State people (quasi equal populated districts).

The "reserved power clause" may be applied in the following two ways to measure the popularity of the Medicare wage tax:

Through the State legislature members "pros and cons" voting

Through the State people voting within "quasi equal populated districts" counting the "pros and cons" of the "quasi equal populated districts"

COMPUTERS MEASURE POPULARITY MEDICARE WAGE TAX

While a Person is balloting in a voting booth, a computer may be used to automatically measure the popularity of the Medicare wage tax. A referendum at election time may be displayed to question the approval or disapproval of the Medicare wage tax. As the person makes a choice in a States polling booth, the computer immediately registers the "pros and cons" responses.

At the end of the day, the computer "pros and cons" responses results are automatically published in the State. The total responses signify the popularity of the Medicare wage tax.

Through using a spread sheet flow chart, a computer may be programmed.

Based upon the counting of "pros and cons" "quasi equal populated districts," "Mob Rule" is eliminated.

Popularity voting the Medicare wage tax will indicate to the States legislature and people within "quasi equal popularity districts" to repeal the Medicare wage tax.

Constitution

Bill of Rights

10th Amendment

Delegated Clause (Constant)
Reserved Power Clause (Popularity Vote Unemployment Tax)

POPULARITY VOTE
Unemployment Wage Tax

The 10th Amendment states "the powers (State) not delegated to the United States by the Constitution, nor prohibited by it (Constitution) to the States (legislature), are reserved (reserved power clause) to the States (legislature) respectively, or to the State people (quasi equal populated districts)."

In other words, "the powers (State) not delegated to the United States by the Constitution, or not prohibited (not allowed) by it (Constitution) to the States (legislature), are reserved (reserved power clause) to the States (legislature) respectively, or to the State people (quasi equal populated districts)."

In other words, "the powers (State) not delegated to the United States by the Constitution, or not _allowed by it (Constitution) to the States (legislature), are reserved (reserved power clause) to the States (legislature) respectively, or to the State people (quasi equal populated districts)."

In other words, "the powers (State) not delegated to the United States by the Constitution, or allowed by it (Constitution) to the States (legislature), are reserved (reserved power clause) to the States (legislature) respectively, or to the State people (quasi equal populated districts)." The "reserved power clause" applies to the States legislature (quasi equal populated districts) or to the State people (quasi equal populated districts). The "reserved power

clause" may be applied in the following two ways to measure the popularity of the Unemployment wage tax:

Through the State legislature members "pros and cons" voting. Through the State people voting within "quasi equal populated districts" counting the "pros and cons" of the "quasi equal populated districts"

COMPUTERS MEASURE POPULARITY UNEMPLOYMENT WAGE TAX

While a Person is balloting in a voting booth, a computer may be used to automatically measure the popularity of the Unemployment wage tax. A referendum at election time may be displayed to question the approval or disapproval of the Unemployment wage tax. As the person makes a choice in a States polling booth, the computer immediately registers the "pros and cons" responses. At the end of the day, the computer "pros and cons" responses results are automatically published in the State. The total responses signify the popularity of the Unemployment wage tax. Through using a spread sheet flow chart, a computer may be programmed. Based upon the counting of "pros and cons" "quasi equal populated districts," "Mob Rule" is eliminated.

Popularity voting the Unemployment wage tax will indicate to the States legislature and people within "quasi equal popularity districts" to repeal the Unemployment wage tax.

MARKET PLACE

(16th Amendment Wage Tax Company)

- Company weekly sends wage taxes to federal
- Government
- Company sends weekly wage tax to the market place
- Company sends snowball taxes to the market place
- Worker pays triple taxes:
- Weekly wage tax
- Snowball sales tax
- Weekly wage sales tax
- Non-worker pays double sales taxes:
- Snowball sales tax
- Weekly wage sales tax
- Government collects triple taxes:
- Weekly wage tax
- Hidden snowball sales tax
- Weekly wage sales tax
- Hidden sales taxes are deposited in treasury.

Products And Services Retain Sales Taxes in Market Place

MARKET PLACE SALES TAXES

The 16th Amendment allows the transmission of the following as sales taxes:

- Company sale tax
- Income sale tax
- Social security wage sale tax
- Medicare wage sale tax
- Unemployment sale tax

Corporations and companies transmit the following taxes to the market place as sales taxes:

- Company tax
- Income tax
- Social security wage tax
- Medicare wage tax
- Unemployment tax

Corporations and companies' taxes convert to sales taxes leading American people to sale tax bondage!!! The 16th Amendment allows a company to transmit to both the Federal government and market place the following taxes:

- Company

- Wage tax
- Social security wage tax
- Medicare wage tax
- Unemployment wage tax
- In the market place, these taxes also are transmitted:
- Snowball Company
- Snowball wage tax
- Snowball Social Security wage tax
- Snowball Medicare wage tax
- Snowball Unemployment wage tax

In the market place, the following taxes are converted to sale taxes:

Company sale taxes:

- Wage sale tax
- Social Security wage sale tax
- Medicare wage sale tax
- Unemployment wage sale tax
- Snowball Company sale tax
- Snowball wage sale tax
- Snowball Social Security wage sale tax
- Snowball Medicare wage sale tax
- Snowball Unemployment wage sale tax

Enslaving the population within the American territory to become sales tax bondage people!!! In any buying sale transaction, non-wage earners as well wage earners pay these sale taxes. The non-wage earners include the following:

- People on Social Security
- People on Medicare
- People on Unemployment
- People using "food stamps"
- People using stimulus money
- People who are tourist
- People of foreign countries buying American products

The people within the United States territory result into paying "multi taxation" where the wage earners pay a "triple tax" and the non-wage earners and foreigners pay a "double tax" on the following sale taxes:

- Company sale tax
- Wage sale tax
- Social security wage sale tax
- Medicare wage sale tax
- Unemployment wage sale tax
- Snowball Company sale tax
- Snowball wage sale tax
- Snowball social security wage sale tax
- Snowball Medicare wage sale tax
- Snowball unemployment wage sale tax

"Reserved Power Clause"

Impeach Judges

(State Judge, County Judge, City Judge, Town Judge, Village Judge)

Constitution

Bill of Rights

10th Amendment

Delegated Clause (Constant)
Reserved Power Clause (Impeach State Judge)

IMPEACH STATE JUDGE

Remove a State Judge

The 10th Amendment states "the powers (State) not delegated to the United States by the Constitution, nor prohibited by it (Constitution) to the States (legislature), are reserved (reserved power clause) to the States (legislature) respectively, or to the State people (quasi equal populated districts)."

In other words, "the powers (State) not delegated to the United States by the Constitution, or not prohibited (not allowed) by it (Constitution) to the States (legislature), are reserved (reserved power clause) to the States (legislature) respectively, or to the State people (quasi equal populated districts)."

In other words, "the powers (State) not delegated to the United States by the Constitution, or not allowed by it (Constitution) to

the States (legislature), are reserved (reserved power clause) to the States (legislature) respectively, or to the State people (quasi equal populated districts)."

In other words, "the powers (State) not delegated to the United States by the Constitution, or allowed by it (Constitution) to the States (legislature), are reserved (reserved power clause) to the States (legislature) respectively, or to the State people (quasi equal populated districts)."

The "reserved power clause" applies to the State legislature (quasi equal populated districts) or to the State people (quasi equal populated districts).

The "reserved power clause" may be applied in the following two ways:

Impeach State judge through the State legislature members voting enforcing 60%-40% rule

Impeach State judge through the State people voting in "quasi equal populated districts" enforcing the 60%-40% rule on the winning districts

The "reserved power clause" is based upon the "power of representation" within State "quasi equal populate districts." Any judgment against the impeach State judge violates the "power of representation" within the State people "quasi equal populated districts."

Constitution

Bill of Rights

10th Amendment

Delegated Clause (Constant)

Reserved Power Clause (Impeach County Judge)

IMPEACH COUNTY JUDGE

Remove a County Judge

The 10th Amendment states "the powers not (County) delegated to the United States by the Constitution, nor prohibited by it (Constitution) to the Counties (legislature), are reserved (reserved power clause) to the Counties (legislature) respectively, or to the County people (quasi equal populated districts)."

In other words, "the powers not (County) delegated to the United States by the Constitution, or not prohibited (not allowed) by it (Constitution) to the Counties (legislature), are reserved (reserved power clause) to the Counties (legislature) respectively, or to the County people (quasi equal populated districts)."

In other words, "the powers not (County) delegated to the United States by the Constitution, or not allowed by it (Constitution) to the Counties (legislature), are reserved (reserved power clause) to

the Counties (legislature) respectively, or to the County people (quasi equal populated districts)."

In other words, "the powers not (County) delegated to the United States by the Constitution, or allowed by it (Constitution) to the Counties (legislature), are reserved (reserved power clause) to the Counties (legislature) respectively, or to the County people (quasi equal populated districts)." The "reserved power clause" applies to the Counties legislature (quasi equal populated districts) or to the County people (quasi equal populated districts).

The "reserved power clause" may be applied in the following two ways:

Through the County legislature where the 60-40 voting prevails counting the number of voting legislature members to impeach a county judge.

Through the County people voting within "quasi equal populated districts" where the 60%-40% rule prevails of counting the number of "quasi equal populated districts" must be in forced to impeach a county judge.

The "reserved power clause" is based upon the "power of representation" within "quasi equal populate districts." Any judgment against the impeach County judge violates the "power of representation" within the County people "quasi equal populated districts"

Constitution

Bill of Rights

10th Amendment

Delegated Clause (Constant)

Reserved Power Clause (Impeach City Judge)

IMPEACH CITY JUDGE

Remove a City Judge

The 10th Amendment states "the powers not (City) delegated to the United States by the Constitution, nor prohibited by it (Constitution) to the Cities (council), are reserved (reserved power clause) to the Cities (council) respectively, or to the city people (quasi equal populated districts)."

In other words, "the powers not (City) delegated to the United States by the Constitution, or not prohibited (not allowed) by it (Constitution) to the Cities (council), are reserved (reserved power clause) to the Cities (council) respectively, or to the city people (quasi equal populated districts)."

In other words, "the powers not (City) delegated to the United States by the Constitution, or not allowed by it (Constitution) to the Cities (council), are reserved (reserved power clause) to the

Cities (council) respectively, or to the city people (quasi equal populated districts)."

In other words, "the powers not (City) delegated to the United States by the Constitution, or allowed by it (Constitution) to the Cities (council), are reserved (reserved power clause) to the Cities (council) respectively, or to the city people (quasi equal populated districts)."

The "reserved power clause" applies to the Cities council (quasi equal populated districts) or to the city people (quasi equal populated districts).

The "reserved power clause" may be applied in the following two ways:

Through the City council where the 60-40 voting prevails counting the number of voting council members to impeach a city judge.

Through the City people voting within "quasi equal populated districts" where the 60%-40% rule prevails of counting the number of "quasi equal populated districts" must be in forced to impeach a city judge.

The "reserved power clause" is based upon the "power of representation" within "quasi equal populate districts."

Any judgment against the impeach City judge violates the "power of representation" within the city people "quasi equal populated districts"

Constitution

Bill of Rights

10th Amendment

Delegated Clause (Constant)

Reserved Power Clause (Impeach Town Judge)

IMPEACH TOWN JUDGE

Remove a Town Judge

The 10th Amendment states "the powers not (Town) delegated to the United States by the Constitution, nor prohibited by it (Constitution) to the Towns (council), are reserved (reserved power clause) to the Towns (council) respectively, or to the Town people (quasi equal populated districts)."

In other words, "the powers not (Town) delegated to the United States by the Constitution, or not prohibited (not allowed) by it (Constitution) to the Towns (council), are reserved (reserved power clause) to the Towns (council) respectively, or to the Town people (quasi equal populated districts)."

In other words, "the powers not (Town) delegated to the United States by the Constitution, or not allowed by it (Constitution) to the Towns (council), are reserved (reserved power clause) to the

Towns (council) respectively, or to the Town people (quasi equal populated districts)."

In other words, "the powers not (Town) delegated to the United States by the Constitution, or allowed by it (Constitution) to the Towns (council), are reserved (reserved power clause) to the Towns (council) respectively, or to the Town people (quasi equal populated districts)." The "reserved power clause" applies to the Town councils (quasi equal populated districts) or to the Town people (quasi equal populated districts).

The "reserved power clause" may be applied in the following two ways:

Through the Town council where the 60-40 voting prevails counting the number of voting council members to impeach a Town judge.

Through the Town people voting within "quasi equal populated districts" where the 60%-40% rule prevails of counting the number of "quasi equal populated districts" must be in forced to impeach a Town judge.

The "reserved power clause" is based upon the "power of representation" within "quasi equal populate districts."

Any judgment against the impeach Town judge violates the "power of representation" within the Town people "quasi equal populated districts"

Constitution

Bill of Rights

10th Amendment

Delegated Clause (Constant)

Reserved Power Clause (Impeach Village Judge)

IMPEACH VILAGE JUDGE

Remove a Village Judge

The 10th Amendment states "the powers not (Village) delegated to the United States by the Constitution, nor prohibited by it (Constitution) to the Villages (council), are reserved (reserved power clause) to the Villages (council) respectively, or to the Village people (quasi equal populated districts)."

In other words, "the powers not (Village) delegated to the United States by the Constitution, or <u>not prohibited (not</u> <u>allowed)</u> by it (Constitution) to the Villages (council), are reserved (reserved power clause) to the Villages (council) respectively, or to the Village people (quasi equal populated districts)."

In other words, "the powers not (Village) delegated to the United States by the Constitution, or <u>not</u> allowed by it (Constitution) to the Villages (council), are reserved (reserved power clause) to the

Villages (council) respectively, or to the Village people (quasi equal populated districts)."

In other words, "the powers not (Village) delegated to the United States by the Constitution, or allowed by it (Constitution) to the Villages (council), are reserved (reserved power clause) to the Villages (council) respectively, or to the Village people (quasi equal populated districts)." The "reserved power clause" applies to the Villages council (quasi equal populated districts) or to the Village people (quasi equal populated districts).

The "reserved power clause" may be applied in the following two ways:

Through the Village council where the 60-40 voting prevails counting the number of voting council members to impeach a Village judge.

Through the Village people voting within "quasi equal populated districts" where the 60%-40% rule prevails of counting the number of "quasi equal populated districts" must be in forced to impeach a Village judge.

The "reserved power clause" is based upon the "power of representation" within "quasi equal populate districts."

Any judgment against the impeach Village judge violates the "power of representation" within the Village people "quasi equal populated districts"

"Reserved Power Clause"

Elections

(State Governor, County Executive, City Mayor, Town Mayor, Village Mayor, House Leader)

Constitution

Bill of Rights

10th Amendment

Delegated Clause (Constant)

Reserved Power Clause (Elect State Governor)

RESERVE POWER CLAUSE

Elect State Governor

The 10th Amendment states "the powers (State) not delegated to the United States by the Constitution, nor prohibited by it (Constitution) to the States (legislature), are reserved (reserved power clause) to the States (legislature) respectively, or to the State people (quasi equal populated districts)."

In other words, "the powers (State) not delegated to the United States by the Constitution, or not prohibited (not allowed) by it (Constitution) to the States (legislature), are reserved (reserved power clause) to the States (legislature) respectively, or to the State people (quasi equal populated districts)."

In other words, "the powers (State) not delegated to the United States by the Constitution, or not allowed by it (Constitution) to the States (legislature), are reserved (reserved power clause) to the

States (legislature) respectively, or to the State people (quasi equal populated districts)."

In other words, "the powers (State) not delegated to the United States by the Constitution, or allowed by it (Constitution) to the States (legislature), are reserved (reserved power clause) to the States (legislature) respectively, or to the State people (quasi equal populated districts)."

The "reserved power clause" applies to the States legislature (quasi equal populated districts) or to the State people "quasi equal populated districts". The "reserved power clause" is applied through the State people "quasi equal populated districts" where the State people voting within the "quasi equal populated districts" elect a state governor eliminating "Mob Rule". The State governor candidate receiving the highest number of votes wins the "quasi equal populated district." The candidate winning the "quasi equal populated districts" wins the election.

In case of a tie vote, the "reserved power clause" turns the voting to the State legislature where the candidate receiving the greatest number of votes wins the election.

In elections, the "reserved power clause" is based upon the "power of representation" within "quasi equal populate districts."

Any judgment against the election of the State governor violates the "power of representation" within the State people "quasi equal populated districts."

Constitution

Bill of Rights

10th Amendment

Delegated Clause (Constant)

Reserved Power Clause (Elect County Executive)

RESERVE POWER CLAUSE

Elect County Executive

The 10th Amendment states "the powers (County) not delegated to the United States by the Constitution, nor prohibited by it (Constitution) to the Counties (legislature), are reserved (reserved power clause) to the Counties (legislature) respectively, or to the County people (quasi equal populated districts)."

In other words, "the powers (County) not delegated to the United States by the Constitution, or not prohibited (not allowed) by it (Constitution) to the Counties (legislature), are reserved (reserved power clause) to the Counties (legislature) respectively, or to the County people (quasi equal populated districts)."

In other words, "the powers (County) not delegated to the United States by the Constitution, or not allowed by it (Constitution) to the Counties (legislature), are reserved (reserved power clause) to

the Counties (legislature) respectively, or to the County people (quasi equal populated districts)."

In other words, "the powers (County) not delegated to the United States by the Constitution, or allowed by it (Constitution) to the Counties (legislature), are reserved (reserved power clause) to the Counties (legislature) respectively, or to the County people (quasi equal populated districts)." The "reserved power clause" applies to the Counties legislature (quasi equal populated districts) or to the County people "quasi equal populated districts".

The "reserved power clause" is applied through the County people "quasi equal populated districts" where the County people voting within the "quasi equal populated districts" elect a county executive eliminating "Mob Rule". The County executive candidate receiving the highest number of votes wins the "quasi equal populated district." The candidate winning the "quasi equal populated districts" wins the election.

In case of a tie vote, the "reserved power clause" turns the voting to the County legislature where the candidate receiving the greatest number of votes wins the election.

In elections, the "reserved power clause" is based upon the "power of representation" within "quasi equal populate districts."

Any judgment against the election of the County executive violates the "power of representation" within the County people "quasi equal populated districts."

Constitution

Bill of Rights

10th Amendment

Delegated Clause (Constant)

Reserved Power Clause (Elect City Mayor)

RESERVE POWER CLAUSE

Elect City Mayor

The 10th Amendment states "the powers (City) not delegated to the United States by the Constitution, nor prohibited by it (Constitution) to the Cities (council), are reserved (reserved power clause) to the Cities (council) respectively, or to the city people (quasi equal populated districts)."

In other words, "the powers (City) not delegated to the United States by the Constitution, or not prohibited (not allowed) by it (Constitution) to the Cities (council), are reserved (reserved power clause) to the Cities (council) respectively, or to the city people (quasi equal populated districts)."

In other words, "the powers (City) not delegated to the United States by the Constitution, or not allowed by it (Constitution) to the Cities (council), are reserved (reserved power clause) to the

Cities (council) respectively, or to the city people (quasi equal populated districts)."

In other words, "the powers (City) not delegated to the United States by the Constitution, or allowed by it (Constitution) to the Cities (council), are reserved (reserved power clause) to the Cities (council) respectively, or to the city people (quasi equal populated districts)." The "reserved power clause" applies to the Cities council (quasi equal populated districts) or to the city people "quasi equal populated districts".

The "reserved power clause" is applied through the City people "quasi equal populated districts" where the City people voting within the "quasi equal populated districts" elect a city mayor eliminating "Mob Rule". The city mayor candidate receiving the highest number of votes wins the "quasi equal populated district." The candidate winning the "quasi equal populated districts" wins the election.

In case of a tie vote, the "reserved power clause" turns the voting to the city council where the candidate receiving the greatest number of votes wins the election.

In elections, the "reserved power clause" is based upon the "power of representation" within "quasi equal populate districts."

Any judgment against the election of the city mayor violates the "power of representation" within the city people "quasi equal populated districts."

Constitution

Bill of Rights

10th Amendment

Delegated Clause (Constant)

Reserved Power Clause (Elect Town Mayor)

RESERVE POWER CLAUSE

Elect Town Mayor

The 10th Amendment states "the powers (Town) not delegated to the United States by the Constitution, nor prohibited by it (Constitution) to the Towns (council), are reserved (reserved power clause) to the Towns (council) respectively, or to the Town people (quasi equal populated districts)."

In other words, "the powers (Town) not delegated to the United States by the Constitution, or not prohibited (not allowed) by it (Constitution) to the Towns (council), are reserved (reserved power clause) to the Towns (council) respectively, or to the Town people (quasi equal populated districts)."

In other words, "the powers (Town) not delegated to the United States by the Constitution, or not allowed by it (Constitution) to the Towns (council), are reserved (reserved power clause) to the

Towns (council) respectively, or to the Town people (quasi equal populated districts)."

In other words, "the powers (Town) not delegated to the United States by the Constitution, or allowed by it (Constitution) to the Towns (council), are reserved (reserved power clause) to the Towns (council) respectively, or to the Town people (quasi equal populated districts)." The "reserved power clause" applies to the Towns council (quasi equal populated districts) or to the Town people "quasi equal populated districts".

The "reserved power clause" is applied through the Town people "quasi equal populated districts" where the Town people voting within the "quasi equal populated districts" elect a Town mayor eliminating "Mob Rule". The Town mayor candidate receiving the highest number of votes wins the "quasi equal populated district." The candidate winning the "quasi equal populated districts" wins the election.

In case of a tie vote, the "reserved power clause" turns the voting to the Town council where the candidate receiving the greatest number of votes wins the election.

In elections, the "reserved power clause" is based upon the "power of representation" within "quasi equal populate districts."

Any judgment against the election of the Town mayor violates the "power of representation" within the Town people "quasi equal populated districts."

Constitution

Bill of Rights

10th Amendment

Delegated Clause (Constant)
Reserved Power Clause (Elect Village Mayor)

RESERVE POWER CLAUSE

Elect Village Mayor

The 10th Amendment states "the powers (Village) not delegated to the United States by the Constitution, nor prohibited by it (Constitution) to the Villages (council), are reserved (reserved power clause) to the Villages (council) respectively, or to the Village people (quasi equal populated districts)."

In other words, "the powers (Village) not delegated to the United States by the Constitution, or not prohibited (not allowed) by it (Constitution) to the Villages (council), are reserved (reserved power clause) to the Villages (council) respectively, or to the Village people (quasi equal populated districts)."

In other words, "the powers (Village) not delegated to the United States by the Constitution, or not allowed by it (Constitution) to the Villages (council), are reserved (reserved power clause) to the

Villages (council) respectively, or to the Village people (quasi equal populated districts)."

In other words, "the powers (Village) not delegated to the United States by the Constitution, or allowed by it (Constitution) to the Villages (council), are reserved (reserved power clause) to the Villages (council) respectively, or to the Village people (quasi equal populated districts)." The "reserved power clause" applies to the Villages council (quasi equal populated districts) or to the Village people "quasi equal populated districts".

The "reserved power clause" is applied through the Village people "quasi equal populated districts" where the Village people voting within the "quasi equal populated districts" elect a Village mayor eliminating "Mob Rule". The Village mayor candidate receiving the highest number of votes wins the "quasi equal populated district." The candidate winning the "quasi equal populated districts" wins the election.

In case of a tie vote, the "reserved power clause" turns the voting to the Village council where the candidate receiving the greatest number of votes wins the election.

In elections, the "reserved power clause" is based upon the "power of representation" within "quasi equal populate districts."

Any judgment against the election of the Village mayor violates the "power of representation" within the Village people "quasi equal populated districts."

Constitution

Bill of Rights

10th Amendment

Delegated Clause (Constant)
Reserved Power Clause (Elect House Leader)

RESERVE POWER CLAUSE

Elect House Leader

The 10th Amendment states "the powers (House) not delegated to the United States by the Constitution, nor prohibited by it (Constitution) to the Houses (legislature), are reserved (reserved power clause) to the Houses (legislature) respectively, or to the House people (quasi equal populated districts)."

In other words, "the powers (House) not delegated to the United States by the Constitution, or not prohibited (not allowed) by it (Constitution) to the Houses (legislature), are reserved (reserved power clause) to the Houses (legislature) respectively, or to the House people (quasi equal populated districts)."

In other words, "the powers (House) not delegated to the United States by the Constitution, or not allowed by it (Constitution) to the Houses (legislature), are reserved (reserved power clause) to

the Houses (legislature) respectively, or to the House people (quasi equal populated districts)."

In other words, "the powers (House) not delegated to the United States by the Constitution, or allowed by it (Constitution) to the Houses (legislature), are reserved (reserved power clause) to the Houses (legislature) respectively, or to the House people (quasi equal populated districts)." The "reserved power clause" applies to the Houses legislature (quasi equal populated districts) or to the House people "quasi equal populated districts".

The "reserved power clause" is applied through the House people "quasi equal populated districts" where the House people voting within the "quasi equal populated districts" elect a House leader eliminating "Mob Rule". The House Leader candidate receiving the highest number of votes wins the "quasi equal populated district." The candidate winning the "quasi equal populated districts" wins the election.

In case of a tie vote, the "reserved power clause" turns the voting to the House legislature where the candidate receiving the greatest number of votes wins the election.

In elections, the "reserved power clause" is based upon the "power of representation" within "quasi equal populate districts."

Any judgment against the election of the House leader violates the "power of representation" within the House people "quasi equal populated districts."

“Reserved Power Clause”

Litigation Amendment

(State, County, City, Town, Village Mayor)

Constitution

Bill of Rights

10th Amendment

Delegated Clause (Constant)

Reserved Power Clause (State Litigation Amendment)

STATE LITIGATION AMENDMENT

Replaces Legal Action State Government Refuses to Perform

A precursor to a republic form of government is the construction of "quasi equal populated districts" throughout a state territory using census data taken every ten years. Elected representative of contiguous State people "quasi equal populated districts" are the members whom ultimately become a proportional representative body in the State legislature guaranteeing ruling through the State people "power of representation" satisfying the "reserved power clause." The State becomes a republic form of government ruling in a bottom-up mode of representation starting at the State people "quasi equal populated districts" and ending at the State governor. The State citizens of those State people "quasi equal populated districts" choose the best leaders among the State people in the "quasi equal populated districts" to influence the legislature in ruling by law protecting the State and State people sovereignty.

The 10th Amendment states, the powers (State) not delegate to the United States by the Constitution, nor prohibited by it (Constitution) to the States (legislature), are (reserved power clause) reserved to the States (legislature) respectively, or to State people (quasi equal populated districts).

In other words, "the powers (State) not delegated to the United States by the constitution, or not prohibited (not allowed) by it (Constitution) to the States (legislature), are reserved to the States (legislature) respectively or to the State people (quasi equal populated districts)."

In other words, "the powers (State) not delegated to the United States by the constitution, or not allowed by it (Constitution) to the States (legislature) are reserved to the States (legislature) respectively or to the State people (quasi equal populated districts)."

In other words, the powers (State) not delegated to the United States by the constitution or allowed by it (Constitution) to the States (legislature) are reserved (reserved power clause) to the States (legislature) respectively or to the State people (quasi equal populated districts).

The "reserved power clause" applies to the State legislature (representing quasi equal populated districts) or to the State people (quasi equal populated districts).

The "reserved power clause" may be applied in the following two ways:

Through the State legislature where the 60-40 voting prevails counting the number of voting legislature representatives

Through the State people voting in State people "quasi equal populated districts" where the 60-40 voting prevails counting the number of those winning State people "quasi equal populated districts"

The "reserved power clause" is based upon the "power of representation" within the State people "quasi equal populate districts." Any judgment against the "State litigation Amendment" violates the people within the State "quasi equal populated districts" "power of representation".

Constitution

Bill of Rights

10th Amendment

Delegated Clause (Constant)

Reserved Power Clause (County Litigation Amendment)

COUNTY LITIGATION AMENDMENT

Replaces Legal Action County Government Refuses to Perform

A precursor to a republic form of government is the construction of "quasi equal populated districts" throughout a county territory using census data taken every ten years. Elected representative of contiguous County people "quasi equal populated districts" are the members whom ultimately become a proportional representative body in the County legislature guaranteeing ruling through the County people "power of representation" satisfying the "reserved power clause." The County becomes a republic form of government ruling in a bottom up mode of representation starting at the County people "quasi equal populated districts" and ending at the County executive. The County citizens of those County people "quasi equal populated districts" choose the best leaders among the County people in the "quasi equal populated districts" to influence the legislature in ruling by law protecting the County and County people sovereignty.

The 10th Amendment states, the powers (County) not delegate to the United States by the Constitution, nor prohibited by it (Constitution) to the Counties (legislature), are (reserved power clause) reserved to the Counties (legislature) respectively, or to County people (quasi equal populated districts).

In other words, "the powers (County) not delegated to the United States by the constitution, or not prohibited (not allowed) by it (Constitution) to the Counties (legislature), are reserved to the Counties (legislature) respectively or to the County people (quasi equal populated districts)."

In other words, "the powers (County) not delegated to the United States by the constitution, or not allowed by it (Constitution) to the Counties (legislature) are reserved to the Counties (legislature) respectively or to the County people (quasi equal populated districts)."

In other words, the powers (County) not delegated to the United States by the constitution or allowed by it (Constitution) to the Counties (legislature) are reserved (reserved power clause) to the Counties (legislature) respectively or to the County people (quasi equal populated districts).

The "reserved power clause" applies to the County legislature (representing quasi equal populated districts) or to the County people (quasi equal populated districts).

The "reserved power clause" may be applied in the following two ways:

Through the County legislature where the 60-40 voting prevails counting the number of voting legislature representatives

Through the County people voting in County people "quasi equal populated districts" where the 60-40 voting prevails counting the number of those winning County people "quasi equal populated districts"

The "reserved power clause" is based upon the "power of representation" within the County people "quasi equal populate districts." Any judgment against the "County litigation Amendment" violates the people within the County "quasi equal populated districts" "power of representation".

Constitution

Bill of Rights

10th Amendment

Delegated Clause (Constant)

Reserved Power Clause (City Litigation Amendment)

CITY LITIGATION AMENDMENT

Replaces Legal Action City Government Refuses to Perform

A precursor to a republic form of government is the construction of "quasi equal populated districts" throughout a city territory using census data taken every ten years. Elected representative of contiguous City people "quasi equal populated districts" are the members whom ultimately become a proportional representative body in the city council guaranteeing ruling through the city people "power of representation" satisfying the "reserved power clause." The City becomes a republic form of government ruling in a bottom-up mode of representation starting at the City people "quasi equal populated districts" and ending at the City mayor. The city citizens of those City people "quasi equal populated districts" choose the best leaders among the city people in the "quasi equal populated districts" to influence the council in ruling by law protecting the City and City people sovereignty. The 10th

Amendment states, the powers (City) not delegate to the United States by the Constitution, nor prohibited by it (Constitution) to the Cities (council), are (reserved power clause) reserved to the Cities (council) respectively, or to City people (quasi equal populated districts).

In other words, "the powers (City) not delegated to the United States by the constitution, or not prohibited (not allowed) by it (Constitution) to the Cities (council), are reserved to the Cities (council) respectively or to the city people (quasi equal populated districts)."

In other words, "the powers (City) not delegated to the United States by the constitution, or not allowed by it (Constitution) to the Cities (council) are reserved to the Cities (council) respectively or to the city people (quasi equal populated districts)."

In other words, the powers (City) not delegated to the United States by the constitution or allowed by it (Constitution) to the Cities (council) are reserved (reserved power clause) to the Cities (council) respectively or to the city people (quasi equal populated districts).

The "reserved power clause" applies to the city council (quasi equal populated districts) or to the city people (quasi equal populated districts).

The "reserved power clause" may be applied in the following two ways:

Through the City council where the 60-40 voting prevails counting the number of voting council representatives

Through the City people voting in City people "quasi equal populated districts" where the 60-40 voting prevails counting the number of those winning City people "quasi equal populated districts"

The "reserved power clause" is based upon the "power of representation" within the City people "quasi equal populate districts." Any judgment against the "City litigation Amendment" violates the people within the city "quasi equal populated districts" "power of representation".

Constitution

Bill of Rights

10th Amendment

Delegated Clause (Constant)

Reserved Power Clause (Town Litigation Amendment)

TOWN LITIGATION AMENDMENT

Replaces Legal Action Town Government Refuses to Perform

A precursor to a republic form of government is the construction of "quasi equal populated districts" throughout a Town territory using census data taken every ten years. Elected representative of contiguous Town people "quasi equal populated districts" are the members whom ultimately become a proportional representative body in the Town council guaranteeing ruling through the Town people "power of representation" satisfying the "reserved power clause." The Town becomes a republic form of government ruling in a bottom-up mode of representation starting at the Town people "quasi equal populated districts" and ending at the Town mayor. The Town citizens of those Town people "quasi equal populated districts" choose the best leaders among the Town people in the "quasi equal populated districts" to influence the council in ruling by law protecting the Town and Town people sovereignty.

The 10th Amendment states, the powers (Town) not delegate to the United States by the Constitution, nor prohibited by it (Constitution) to the Towns (council), are (reserved power clause) reserved to the Towns (council) respectively, or to Town people (quasi equal populated districts).

In other words, "the powers (Town) not delegated to the United States by the constitution, or not prohibited (not allowed) by it (Constitution) to the Towns (council), are reserved to the Towns (council) respectively or to the Town people (quasi equal populated districts)."

In other words, "the powers (Town) not delegated to the United States by the constitution, or not allowed by it (Constitution) to the Towns (council) are reserved to the Towns (council) respectively or to the Town people (quasi equal populated districts)."

In other words, the powers (Town) not delegated to the United States by the constitution or allowed by it (Constitution) to the Towns (council) are reserved (reserved power clause) to the Towns (council) respectively or to the Town people (quasi equal populated districts).

The "reserved power clause" applies to the Town council (representing quasi equal populated districts) or to the Town people (quasi equal populated districts).

The "reserved power clause" may be applied in the following two ways:

Through the Town council where the 60-40 voting prevails counting the number of voting council representatives

Through the Town people voting in Town people "quasi equal populated districts" where the 60-40 voting prevails counting the number of those winning Town people "quasi equal populated districts"

The "reserved power clause" is based upon the "power of representation" within the Town people "quasi equal populate districts." Any judgment against the "Town litigation Amendment" violates the people within the Town people "quasi equal populated districts" "power of representation".

Constitution

Bill of Rights

10th Amendment

Delegated Clause (Constant)
Reserved Power Clause (Village Litigation Amendment)

VILLAGE LITIGATION AMENDMENT

Replaces Legal Action Village Government Refuses to Perform

A precursor to a republic form of government is the construction of "quasi equal populated districts" throughout a Village territory using census data taken every ten years. Elected representative of contiguous Village people "quasi equal populated districts" are the members whom ultimately become a proportional representative body in the Village council guaranteeing ruling through the Village people "power of representation" satisfying the "reserved power clause." The Village becomes a republic form of government ruling in a bottom-up mode of representation starting at the Village people "quasi equal populated districts" and ending at the Village mayor. The Village citizens of those Village people "quasi equal populated districts" choose the best leaders among the Village people in the "quasi equal populated districts" to influence the council in ruling by law protecting the Village and Village people sovereignty.

The 10th Amendment states, the powers (Village) not delegate to the United States by the Constitution, nor prohibited by it (Constitution) to the Villages (council), are (reserved power clause) reserved to the Villages (council) respectively, or to Village people (quasi equal populated districts).

In other words, "the powers (Village) not delegated to the United States by the constitution, or not prohibited (not allowed) by it (Constitution) to the Villages (council), are reserved to the Villages (council) respectively or to the Village people (quasi equal populated districts)."

In other words, "the powers (Village) not delegated to the United States by the constitution, or not allowed by it (Constitution) to the Villages (council) are reserved to the Villages (council) respectively or to the Village people (quasi equal populated districts)."

In other words, the powers (Village) not delegated to the United States by the constitution or allowed by it (Constitution) to the Villages (council) are reserved (reserved power clause) to the Villages (council) respectively or to the Village people (quasi equal populated districts).

The "reserved power clause" applies to the Village council (representing quasi equal populated districts) or to the Village people (quasi equal populated districts).

The "reserved power clause" may be applied in the following two ways:

Through the Village council where the 60-40 voting prevails counting the number of voting council representatives

Through the Village people voting in Village people "quasi equal populated districts" where the 60-40 voting prevails counting the number of those winning Village people "quasi equal populated districts"

The "reserved power clause" is based upon the "power of representation" within the Village people "quasi equal populate districts." Any judgment against the "Village litigation Amendment" violates the people within the Village "quasi equal populated districts" "power of representation".

"REPUBLIC FORM OF GOVERNMENT"

- State legislature elects United States senators.
- "Quasi equal populated districts" represent United States senators.
- "Quasi equal populated districts" represent House of Representatives.
- (Bicameral legislature)

UNITED STATES GOVERNMENT DEMOCRATIC FORM OF GOVERNMENT

17th Amendment had people elect senators. The 17th Amendment took away the State "quasi equal populated districts" "power of representation". The United State Senate usurps States governments' legislature power. Repeal the 17th amendment!!!

ARTICLE V

IMPEACHMENT OF THE UNITED STATES PRESIDENT

- President
- Cabinet Members
- United States Judges

REPEALS

- 16th Amendment
- 17th Amendment
- Roe v. Wade
- Same-Sex Marriage
- Federal Reserve Act
- No Child Left Behind

NATIONAL SECURITY

- National Security Agency

EXECUTIVE AUTHORITY

- Executive Orders

Constitution

Bill of Rights

10th Amendment

Delegated Clause (Article V)
Article V Impeach (US President)

ARTICLE V IMPEACH
United States President

The Congress, whenever two thirds of both Houses shall deem it necessary, shall propose (Impeach President) Amendments to this Constitution, or, on the application of the Legislature of two thirds of the several States, shall call a Convention for proposing (Impeach President) Amendments, which, in either Case, shall be valid to all Intents and Purposes, as Part of this Constitution, when ratified by the Legislature of three fourths of the several

States, or by Conventions in three fourths thereof, as the one or the other Mode of Ratification may be proposed by the Congress…

Constitution

Bill of Rights

10th Amendment

Delegated Clause (Article V)

Article V Impeach (President Cabinet Member)

ARTICLE V IMPEACH

United States President Cabinet Member

The Congress, whenever two thirds of both Houses shall deem it necessary, shall propose (Impeach President cabinet member) Amendments to this Constitution, or, on the application of the Legislature of two thirds of the several States, shall call a Convention for proposing (Impeach President cabinet member) Amendments, which, in either Case, shall be valid to all Intents and Purposes, as Part of

this Constitution, when ratified by the Legislature of three fourths of the several States, or by Conventions in three fourths thereof, as the one or the other Mode of Ratification may be proposed by the Congress…

CABINET MEMBERS

- Vice President Department of State
- Department of the Treasury
- Department of Defense
- Department of Justice
- Department of the Interior
- Department of Agriculture
- Department of Commerce
- Department of Labor
- Department of Health and Human Services
- Department of Housing and Urban Development
- Department of Transportation
- Department of Energy Secretary Ernest
- Moniz Department of Education
- Department of Veterans Affairs
- Department of Homeland Security

Constitution

Bill of Rights

10th Amendment

Delegated Clause (Article V)
Article V Impeach (US Judge)

ARTICLE V IMPEACH

United States President Cabinet Member

The Congress, whenever two thirds of both Houses shall deem it necessary, shall propose (Impeach United States Judge) Amendments to this Constitution, or, on the application of the Legislature of two thirds of the several States, shall call a Convention for proposing (Impeach United States Judge) Amendments, which, in either Case, shall be valid to all Intents and Purposes, as Part of this Constitution, when ratified by the Legislature of three fourths of the several States, or by Conventions in three fourths thereof, as the one or the other Mode of Ratification may be proposed by the Congress…

Constitution

Bill of Rights

10th Amendment

Delegated Clause (Article V)

Article V Repeal (16th Amendment)

ARTICLE V REPEAL 16th AMENDMENT

The Congress, whenever two thirds of both Houses shall deem it necessary, shall propose (Repeal 16th Amendment) Amendments to this Constitution, or, on the application of the Legislature of two thirds of the several States, shall call a Convention for proposing (Repeal 16th Amendment) Amendments, which, in either Case, shall be valid to all Intents and Purposes, as Part of this Constitution, when ratified by the Legislature of three fourths of the several States, or by Conventions in three fourths thereof, as the one or the other Mode of Ratification may be proposed by the Congress…

Constitution

Bill of Rights

10th Amendment

Delegated Clause (Article V)

Article V Repeal (17th Amendment)

ARTICLE V REPEAL 17th AMENDMENT

The Congress, whenever two thirds of both Houses shall deem it necessary, shall propose (Repeal 17th Amendment) Amendments to this Constitution, or, on the application of the Legislature of two thirds of the several States, shall call a Convention for proposing (Repeal 17th Amendment) Amendments, which, in either Case, shall be valid to all Intents and Purposes, as Part of this Constitution, when ratified by the Legislature of three fourths of the several States, or by Conventions in three fourths thereof, as the one or the other Mode of Ratification may be proposed by the Congress…

Constitution

Bill of Rights

10th Amendment

Delegated Clause (Article V)
Repeal (Roe Versus Wade)

ARTICLE V REPEAL ROE VERSUS WADE

The Congress, whenever two thirds of both Houses shall deem it necessary, shall propose (Repeal Roe Versus Wade) Amendments to this Constitution, or, on the application of the Legislature of two thirds of the several States, shall call a Convention for proposing (Repeal Roe Versus Wade) Amendments, which, in either Case, shall be valid to all Intents and Purposes, as Part of this Constitution, when ratified by the Legislature of three fourths of the several States, or by Conventions in three fourths thereof, as the one or the other Mode of Ratification may be proposed by the Congress…

Constitution

Bill of Rights

10th Amendment

Delegated Clause (Article V)

Repeal (Roe Versus Wade)

ARTICLE V REPEAL SAME SEX MARRIAGE

The Congress, whenever two thirds of both Houses shall deem it necessary, shall propose (Repeal same sex marriage) Amendments to this Constitution, or, on the application of the Legislature of two thirds of the several States, shall call a Convention for proposing (Repeal same sex marriage) Amendments, which, in either Case, shall be valid to all Intents and Purposes, as Part of this Constitution, when ratified by the Legislature of three fourths of the several States, or by Conventions in three fourths thereof, as the one or the other Mode of Ratification may be proposed by the Congress...

Constitution

Bill of Rights

10th Amendment

Delegated Clause (Article V)
Repeal (Federal Reserve Act)

ARTICLE V REPEAL FEDERAL RESERVE ACT

The Congress, whenever two thirds of both Houses shall deem it necessary, shall propose (Repeal Federal Reserve Act) Amendments to this Constitution, or, on the application of the Legislature of two thirds of the several States, shall call a Convention for proposing (Repeal Federal Reserve Act) Amendments, which, in either Case, shall be valid to all Intents and Purposes, as Part of this Constitution, when ratified by the Legislature of three fourths of the several States, or by Conventions in three fourths thereof, as the one or the other Mode of Ratification may be proposed by the Congress…

Constitution

Bill of Rights

10th Amendment

Delegated Clause (Article V)
Repeal (No Child Left Behind)

ARTICLE V REPEAL NO CHILD LEFT BEHIND

The Congress, whenever two thirds of both Houses shall deem it necessary, shall propose (Repeal no child left behind) Amendments to this Constitution, or, on the application of the Legislature of two thirds of the several States, shall call a Convention for proposing (Repeal no child left behind) Amendments, which, in either Case, shall be valid to all Intents and Purposes, as Part of this Constitution, when ratified by the Legislature of three fourths of the several.

States, or by Conventions in three fourths thereof, as the one or the other Mode of Ratification may be proposed by the Congress…

Constitution

Bill of Rights

10th Amendment

Delegated Clause (Article V)

Repeal (National Security Agency)

ARTICLE V REPEAL NATIONAL SECURITY AGENCY

The Congress, whenever two thirds of both Houses shall deem it necessary, shall propose (Repeal National Security Agency) Amendments to this Constitution, or, on the application of the Legislature of two thirds of the several States, shall call a Convention for proposing (Repeal National Security Agency) Amendments, which, in either Case, shall be valid to all Intents and Purposes, as Part of this Constitution, when ratified by the Legislature of three fourths of the several States, or by Conventions in three fourths thereof, as the one or the other Mode of Ratification may be proposed by the Congress…

Constitution

Bill of Rights

10th Amendment

Delegated Clause (Article V)

Repeal (Executive Order)

ARTICLE V REPEAL Executive Order

The Congress, whenever two thirds of both Houses shall deem it necessary, shall propose (Repeal executive order) Amendments to this Constitution, or, on the application of the Legislature of two thirds of the several States, shall call a Convention for proposing (Repeal executive order) Amendments, which, in either Case, shall be valid to all Intents and Purposes, as Part of this Constitution, when ratified by the Legislature of three fourths of the several States, or by Conventions in three fourths thereof, as the one or the other Mode of Ratification may be proposed by the Congress...

“ARTICLE V”

- ADD ABORTION
- REPEAL ABORTION

Constitution

Bill of Rights

10th Amendment

Delegated Clause (Article V)

Article V (Add Abortion)

ARTICLE V ADD ABORTION

The Congress, whenever two thirds of both Houses shall deem it necessary, shall propose (Add Abortion) Amendments to this Constitution, or, on the application of the Legislature of two thirds of the several States, shall call a Convention for proposing (Add Abortion) Amendments, which, in either Case, shall be valid to all Intents and Purposes, as Part of this Constitution, when ratified by the Legislature of three fourths of the several States, or by Conventions in three fourths thereof, as the one or the other Mode of Ratification may be proposed by the Congress…

Constitution

Bill of Rights

10th Amendment

Delegated Clause (Article V)
Article V Repeal (Abortion)

ARTICLE V REPEAL ABORTION

The Congress, whenever two thirds of both Houses shall deem it necessary, shall propose (Repeal Abortion) Amendments to this Constitution, <u>or</u>, on the application of the Legislature of two thirds of the several States, shall call a Convention for proposing (Repeal Abortion) Amendments, which, in either Case, shall be valid to all Intents and Purposes, as Part of this Constitution, when ratified by the Legislature of three fourths of the several States, or by Conventions in three fourths thereof, as the one or the other Mode of Ratification may be proposed by the Congress…

EXECUTIVE ORDER SHOULD IMPEACH THE PRESIDENT

EXCUTIVE ORDER

Presidential executive order voids ARTICLE V nullifying Congress. The President becomes a dictator and must be impeached. The Revolutionary War was fought over the "power of representation"." The executive order violates the "power of representation" within "quasi equal populated districts." The planners of the Constitution did not give power to an individual.

DEMOCRACIES VIOLATE

"RESERVED POWER CLAUSE"
AND
"DESIGNATE MOB RULE"

“Reserved Power Clause”

Addition Right to Life Amendment

(State, County, City, Town, Village)

Constitution

Bill of Rights

10th Amendment

Delegated Clause (Constant)
Reserve Power Clause (State Add Right to Life Amendment)

RESERVE POWER CLAUSE
State Add Right to Life Amendment

(A State government has the power to add a "right to life" amendment.)

The 10th Amendment states "the powers (State) not delegated to the United States by the Constitution, nor prohibited by it (Constitution) to the States (legislature), are reserved (reserved power clause) to the States (legislature) respectively, or to the State people (quasi equal populated districts)."

In other words, "the powers (State) not delegated to the United States by the Constitution, or <u>not prohibited</u> (not allowed) by it (Constitution) to the States (legislature), are reserved (reserved power clause) to the States (legislature) respectively, or to the State people (quasi equal populated districts)."

In other words, "the powers (State) not delegated to the United States by the Constitution, or not allowed by it (Constitution) to the States (legislature), are reserved (reserved power clause) to the States (legislature) respectively, or to the State people (quasi equal populated districts)."

In other words, "the powers (State) not delegated to the United States by the Constitution, or allowed by it (Constitution) to the States (legislature), are reserved (reserved power clause) to the States (legislature) respectively, or to the State people (quasi equal populated districts)."

The "reserved power clause" applies to the State legislature (quasi equal populated districts) or to the State people (quasi equal populated districts).

The "reserved power clause" may be applied in the following two ways:

Add "right to life amendment" through the State legislature where the 60-40 voting prevails counting the number of voting legislature members

Add "right to life amendment" through the State people voting within "quasi equal populated districts" where the 60%-40% rule prevails of counting the number of winning "quasi equal populated districts" must be in forced to add a State "right to life amendment"

The "reserved power clause" is based upon the "power of representation" within "quasi equal populate districts." Any judgment against the "State add right to life amendment" violates the "power of representation" within the State people "quasi equal populated districts."

Constitution

Bill of Rights

10th Amendment

Delegated Clause (Constant)

Reserve Power Clause (County Add Right to Life Amendment)

RESERVE POWER CLAUSE

County Add Right to Life Amendment

(A County government has the power to add a "right to life" amendment.)

The 10th Amendment states "the powers (County) not delegated to the United States by the Constitution, nor prohibited by it (Constitution) to the Counties (legislature), are reserved (reserved power clause) to the Counties (legislature) respectively, or to the County people (quasi equal populated districts)."

In other words, "the powers (County) not delegated to the United States by the Constitution, or not prohibited (not allowed) by it (Constitution) to the Counties (legislature), are reserved (reserved power clause) to the Counties (legislature) respectively, or to the County people (quasi equal populated districts)."

In other words, "the powers (County) not delegated to the United States by the Constitution, or not allowed by it (Constitution) to the Counties (legislature), are reserved (reserved power clause) to the Counties (legislature) respectively, or to the County people (quasi equal populated districts)."

In other words, "the powers (County) not delegated to the United States by the Constitution, or allowed by it (Constitution) to the Counties (legislature), are reserved (reserved power clause) to the Counties (legislature) respectively, or to the County people (quasi equal populated districts)."

The "reserved power clause" applies to the County legislature (quasi equal populated districts) or to the County people (quasi equal populated districts).

The "reserved power clause" may be applied in the following two ways:

Add "right to life amendment" through the County legislature where the 60-40 voting prevails counting the number of voting legislature members

Add "right to life amendment" through the County people voting within "quasi equal populated districts" where the 60%-40% rule prevails of counting the number of winning "quasi equal populated districts" must be in forced to add a County "right to life amendment"

The "reserved power clause" is based upon the "power of representation" within "quasi equal populate districts." Any judgment against the "County add right to life amendment" violates the "power of representation" within the County people "quasi equal populated districts."

Constitution

Bill of Rights

10th Amendment

Delegated Clause (Constant)

Reserve Power Clause (City Add Right to Life Amendment)

RESERVE POWER CLAUSE
City Add Right to Life Amendment

(A City government has the power to add a "right to life" amendment.)

The 10th Amendment states "the powers (City) not delegated to the United States by the Constitution, nor prohibited by it (Constitution) to the Cities (council), are reserved (reserved power clause) to the Cities (council) respectively, or to the city people (quasi equal populated districts)."

In other words, "the powers (City) not delegated to the United States by the Constitution, or not prohibited (not allowed) by it (Constitution) to the Cities (council), are reserved (reserved power clause) to the Cities (council) respectively, or to the city people (quasi equal populated districts)."

In other words, "the powers (City) not delegated to the United States by the Constitution, or <u>not</u> allowed by it (Constitution) to

the Cities (council), are reserved (reserved power clause) to the Cities (council) respectively, or to the city people (quasi equal populated districts)."

In other words, "the powers (City) not delegated to the United States by the Constitution, or allowed by it (Constitution) to the Cities (council), are reserved (reserved power clause) to the Cities (council) respectively, or to the city people (quasi equal populated districts)." The "reserved power clause" applies to the city council (quasi equal populated districts) or to the city people (quasi equal populated districts).

The "reserved power clause" may be applied in the following two ways:

Add "right to life amendment" through the City council where the 60-40 voting prevails counting the number of voting council members

Add "right to life amendment" through the City people voting within "quasi equal populated districts" where the 60%-40% rule prevails of counting the number of winning "quasi equal populated districts" must be in forced to add a city amendment

The "reserved power clause" is based upon the "power of representation" within "quasi equal populate districts." Any judgment against the "City add right to life amendment" violates the "power of representation" within the City people "quasi equal populated districts."

Constitution

Bill of Rights

10th Amendment

Delegated Clause (Constant)

Reserve Power Clause (Town Add Right to Life Amendment)

RESERVE POWER CLAUSE
Town Add Right to Life Amendment

(A Town government has the power to add a "right to life" amendment.)

The 10th Amendment states "the powers (Town) not delegated to the United States by the Constitution, nor prohibited by it (Constitution) to the Towns (council), are reserved (reserved power clause) to the Towns (council) respectively, or to the Town people (quasi equal populated districts)."

In other words, "the powers (Town) not delegated to the United States by the Constitution, or not prohibited (not allowed) by it (Constitution) to the Towns (council), are reserved (reserved power clause) to the Towns (council) respectively, or to the Town people (quasi equal populated districts)."

In other words, "the powers (Town) not delegated to the United States by the Constitution, or <u>not</u> allowed by it (Constitution) to the Towns (council), are reserved (reserved power clause) to the Towns (council) respectively, or to the Town people (quasi equal populated districts)."

In other words, "the powers (Town) not delegated to the United States by the Constitution, or allowed by it (Constitution) to the Towns (council), are reserved (reserved power clause) to the Towns (council) respectively, or to the Town people (quasi equal populated districts)."

The "reserved power clause" applies to the Town council (quasi equal populated districts) or to the Town people (quasi equal populated districts).

The "reserved power clause" may be applied in the following two ways:

Add "right to life amendment" through the Town council where the 60-40 voting prevails counting the number of voting council members

Add "right to life amendment" through the Town people voting within "quasi equal populated districts" where the 60%-40% rule prevails of counting the number of winning "quasi equal populated districts" must be in forced to add a "Town right to life amendment."

The “reserved power clause” is based upon the “power of representation” within “quasi equal populate districts.” Any judgment against the “Town right to life amendment” violates the “power of representation” within the Town people “quasi equal populated districts.”

Constitution

Bill of Rights

10th Amendment

Delegated Clause (Constant)

Reserve Power Clause (Village Add Right to Life Amendment)

RESERVE POWER CLAUSE
Village Add Right to Life Amendment

(A Village government has the power to add a "right to life" amendment.)

The 10th Amendment states "the powers (Village) not delegated to the United States by the Constitution, nor prohibited by it (Constitution) to the Villages (council), are reserved (reserved power clause) to the Villages (council) respectively, or to the Village people (quasi equal populated districts)."

In other words, "the powers (Village) not delegated to the United States by the Constitution, or not prohibited (not allowed) by it (Constitution) to the Villages (council), are reserved (reserved power clause) to the Villages (council) respectively, or to the Village people (quasi equal populated districts)."

In other words, "the powers (Village) not delegated to the United States by the Constitution, or <u>not</u> allowed by it (Constitution) to the Villages (council), are reserved (reserved power clause) to the Villages (council) respectively, or to the Village people (quasi equal populated districts)."

In other words, "the powers (Village) not delegated to the United States by the Constitution, or allowed by it (Constitution) to the Villages (council), are reserved (reserved power clause) to the Villages (council) respectively, or to the Village people (quasi equal populated districts)."

The "reserved power clause" applies to the Village council (quasi equal populated districts) or to the Village people (quasi equal populated districts).

The "reserved power clause" may be applied in the following two ways:

Add "right to life amendment" through the Village council where the 60-40 voting prevails counting the number of voting council members

Add "right to life amendment" through the Village people voting within "quasi equal populated districts" where the 60%-40% rule prevails of counting the number of winning "quasi equal populated districts" must be in forced to add "right to life amendment."

The "reserved power clause" is based upon the "power of representation" within "quasi equal populate districts." Any

judgment against the "Village add right to life amendment" violates the "power of representation" within the Village people "quasi equal populated districts."

“Reserved Power Clause”

Add Abortion Amendment

(State, County, City, Town, Village)

Constitution

Bill of Rights

10th Amendment

Delegated Clause (Constant)
Reserve Power Clause (State Add Abortion Amendment)

RESERVE POWER CLAUSE
State Add Abortion Amendment

(A State government has the power to add an abortion amendment.)

The 10th Amendment states "the powers (State) not delegated to the United States by the Constitution, nor prohibited by it (Constitution) to the States (legislature), are reserved (reserved power clause) to the States (legislature) respectively, or to the State people (quasi equal populated districts)."

In other words, "the powers (State) not delegated to the United States by the Constitution, or <u>not prohibited</u> (not allowed) by it (Constitution) to the States (legislature), are reserved (reserved power clause) to the States (legislature) respectively, or to the State people (quasi equal populated districts)."

In other words, "the powers (State) not delegated to the United States by the Constitution, or <u>not</u> allowed by it (Constitution) to

the States (legislature), are reserved (reserved power clause) to the States (legislature) respectively, or to the State people (quasi equal populated districts)."

In other words, "the powers (State) not delegated to the United States by the Constitution, or allowed by it (Constitution) to the States (legislature), are reserved (reserved power clause) to the States (legislature) respectively, or to the State people (quasi equal populated districts)." The "reserved power clause" applies to the State legislature (quasi equal populated districts) or to the State people (quasi equal populated districts).

The "reserved power clause" may be applied in the following two ways:

Add "abortion amendment" through the State legislature where the 60-40 voting prevails counting the number of voting legislature members

Add "abortion amendment" through the State people voting within "quasi equal populated districts" where the 60%-40% rule prevails of counting the number of winning "quasi equal populated districts" must be in forced to add a State "abortion amendment"

The "reserved power clause" is based upon the "power of representation" within "quasi equal populate districts." Any judgment against the State "add abortion amendment" violates the "power of representation" within the State people "quasi equal populated districts."

Constitution

Bill of Rights

10th Amendment

Delegated Clause (Constant)
Reserve Power Clause (County Add Abortion Amendment)

RESERVE POWER CLAUSE
County Add Abortion Amendment

(A County government has the power to add an abortion amendment.)

The 10th Amendment states "the powers (County) not delegated to the United States by the Constitution, nor prohibited by it (Constitution) to the Counties (legislature), are reserved (reserved power clause) to the Counties (legislature) respectively, or to the County people (quasi equal populated districts)."

In other words, "the powers (County) not delegated to the United States by the Constitution, or not prohibited (not allowed) by it (Constitution) to the Counties (legislature), are reserved (reserved power clause) to the Counties (legislature) respectively, or to the County people (quasi equal populated districts)."

In other words, "the powers (County) not delegated to the United States by the Constitution, or <u>not</u> allowed by it (Constitution) to the Counties (legislature), are reserved (reserved power clause) to the Counties (legislature) respectively, or to the County people (quasi equal populated districts)."

In other words, "the powers (County) not delegated to the United States by the Constitution, or allowed by it (Constitution) to the Counties (legislature), are reserved (reserved power clause) to the Counties (legislature) respectively, or to the County people (quasi equal populated districts)."

The "reserved power clause" applies to the County legislature (quasi equal populated districts) or to the County people (quasi equal populated districts).

The "reserved power clause" may be applied in the following two ways:

Add "abortion amendment" through the County legislature where the 60-40 voting prevails counting the number of voting legislature members

Add "abortion amendment" through the County people voting within "quasi equal populated districts" where the 60%-40% rule prevails of counting the number of winning "quasi equal populated districts" must be in forced to add a County "abortion amendment."

The "reserved power clause" is based upon the "power of representation" within "quasi equal populate districts." Any judgment against the County "add abortion amendment" violates the “power of representation” within the County people “quasi equal populated districts.”

Constitution

Bill of Rights

10th Amendment

Delegated Clause (Constant)

Reserve Power Clause (City Add Abortion Amendment)

RESERVE POWER CLAUSE
City Add Abortion Amendment

(A City government has the power to add an abortion amendment.)

The 10th Amendment states "the powers (City) not delegated to the United States by the Constitution, nor prohibited by it (Constitution) to the Cities (council), are reserved (reserved power clause) to the Cities (council) respectively, or to the city people (quasi equal populated districts)."

In other words, "the powers (City) not delegated to the United States by the Constitution, or not prohibited (not allowed) by it (Constitution) to the Cities (council), are reserved (reserved power clause) to the Cities (council) respectively, or to the city people (quasi equal populated districts)."

In other words, "the powers (City) not delegated to the United States by the Constitution, or <u>not</u> allowed by it (Constitution) to

the Cities (council), are reserved (reserved power clause) to the Cities (council) respectively, or to the city people (quasi equal populated districts)."

In other words, "the powers (City) not delegated to the United States by the Constitution, or allowed by it (Constitution) to the Cities (council), are reserved (reserved power clause) to the Cities (council) respectively, or to the city people (quasi equal populated districts)."The "reserved power clause" applies to the city council (quasi equal populated districts) or to the city people (quasi equal populated districts).

The "reserved power clause" may be applied in the following two ways:

Add "abortion amendment" through the city council where the 60-40 voting prevails counting the number of voting council members

Add "abortion amendment" through the City people voting within "quasi equal populated districts" where the 60%- 40% rule prevails of counting the number of winning "quasi equal populated districts" must be in forced to add a city "abortion amendment."

The "reserved power clause" is based upon the "power of representation" within "quasi equal populate districts." Any judgment against the city "add abortion amendment" violates the "power of representation" within the city people "quasi equal populated districts."

Constitution

Bill of Rights

10th Amendment

Delegated Clause (Constant)

Reserve Power Clause (Town Add Abortion Amendment)

RESERVE POWER CLAUSE
Town Add Abortion Amendment

(A Town government has the power to add an abortion amendment.)

The 10th Amendment states "the powers (Town) not delegated to the United States by the Constitution, nor prohibited by it (Constitution) to the Towns (council), are reserved (reserved power clause) to the Towns (council) respectively, or to the Town people (quasi equal populated districts)."

In other words, "the powers (Town) not delegated to the United States by the Constitution, or not prohibited (not allowed) by it (Constitution) to the Towns (council), are reserved (reserved power clause) to the Towns (council) respectively, or to the Town people (quasi equal populated districts)."

In other words, "the powers (Town) not delegated to the United States by the Constitution, or <u>not</u> allowed by it (Constitution) to the Towns (council), are reserved (reserved power clause) to the Towns (council) respectively, or to the Town people (quasi equal populated districts)."

In other words, "the powers (Town) not delegated to the United States by the Constitution, or allowed by it (Constitution) to the Towns (council), are reserved (reserved power clause) to the Towns (council) respectively, or to the Town people (quasi equal populated districts)." The "reserved power clause" applies to the Town council (quasi equal populated districts) or to the Town people (quasi equal populated districts).

The "reserved power clause" may be applied in the following two ways:

Add "abortion amendment" through the Town council where the 60-40 voting prevails counting the number of voting council members

Add "abortion amendment" through the Town people voting within "quasi equal populated districts" where the 60%-40% rule prevails of counting the number of winning "quasi equal populated districts" must be in forced to add a Town "abortion amendment."

The "reserved power clause" is based upon the "power of representation" within "quasi equal populate districts." Any judgment against the Town "add abortion amendment" violates the "power of representation" within the Town people "quasi equal populated districts."

Constitution

Bill of Rights

10th Amendment

Delegated Clause (Constant)

Reserve Power Clause (Village Add Abortion Amendment)

RESERVE POWER CLAUSE
Village Add Abortion Amendment

(A Village government has the power to add an abortion amendment.)

The 10th Amendment states "the powers (Village) not delegated to the United States by the Constitution, nor prohibited by it (Constitution) to the Villages (council), are reserved (reserved power clause) to the Villages (council) respectively, or to the Village people (quasi equal populated districts)."

In other words, "the powers (Village) not delegated to the United States by the Constitution, or not prohibited (not allowed) by it (Constitution) to the Villages (council), are reserved (reserved power clause) to the Villages (council) respectively, or to the Village people (quasi equal populated districts)."

In other words, "the powers (Village) not delegated to the United States by the Constitution, or <u>not</u> allowed by it (Constitution) to the Villages (council), are reserved (reserved power clause) to the Villages (council) respectively, or to the Village people (quasi equal populated districts)."

In other words, "the powers (Village) not delegated to the United States by the Constitution, or allowed by it (Constitution) to the Villages (council), are reserved (reserved power clause) to the Villages (council) respectively, or to the Village people (quasi equal populated districts)."

The "reserved power clause" applies to the Village council (quasi equal populated districts) or to the Village people (quasi equal populated districts).

The "reserved power clause" may be applied in the following two ways:

Add "abortion amendment" through the Village council where the 60-40 voting prevails counting the number of voting council members

Add "abortion amendment" through the Village people voting within "quasi equal populated districts" where the 60%-40% rule prevails of counting the number of winning "quasi equal populated districts" must be in forced to add a Village "abortion amendment."

The "reserved power clause" is based upon the "power of representation" within "quasi equal populate districts." Any judgment against the Village "add abortion amendment" violates the "power of representation" within the Village people "quasi equal populated districts."

"Reserved Power Clause"

Right to Life Amendment

(State, County, City, Town, Village)

Constitution

Bill of Rights

10th Amendment

Delegated Clause (Constant)

Reserve Power Clause (Sate Rescind Right to Life Amendment)

RESERVE POWER CLAUSE
Sate Rescind Right to Life Amendment

(A State government has the power to rescind a "right to life" amendment.)

The 10th Amendment states "the powers (State) not delegated to the United States by the Constitution, nor prohibited by it (Constitution) to the States (legislature), are reserved (reserved power clause) to the States (legislature) respectively, or to the State people (quasi equal populated districts)."

In other words, "the powers (State) not delegated to the United States by the Constitution, or not prohibited (not allowed) by it (Constitution) to the States (legislature), are reserved (reserved power clause) to the States (legislature) respectively, or to the State people (quasi equal populated districts)."

In other words, "the powers (State) not delegated to the United States by the Constitution, or not allowed by it (Constitution) to the States (legislature), are reserved (reserved power clause) to the States (legislature) respectively, or to the State people (quasi equal populated districts)."

In other words, "the powers (State) not delegated to the United States by the Constitution, or allowed by it (Constitution) to the States (legislature), are reserved (reserved power clause) to the States (legislature) respectively, or to the State people (quasi equal populated districts)."

The "reserved power clause" applies to the State legislature (quasi equal populated districts) or to the State people (quasi equal populated districts).

The "reserved power clause" may be applied in the following two ways:

Rescind "right to life amendment" through the State legislature where the 60-40 voting prevails counting the number of voting legislature members

Rescind "right to life amendment" through the State people voting within "quasi equal populated districts" where the 60%-40% rule prevails of counting the number of winning "quasi equal populated districts" must be in forced to rescind a State "right to life amendment".

The "reserved power clause" is based upon the "power of representation" within "quasi equal populate districts." Any judgment against the State "rescind right to life amendment" violates the "power of representation" within the State people "quasi equal populated districts."

Constitution

Bill of Rights

10th Amendment

Delegated Clause (Constant)
Reserve Power Clause (County Rescind Right to Life Amendment)

RESERVE POWER CLAUSE
County Rescind Right to Life Amendment

(A County government has the power to rescind a "right to life" amendment.)

The 10th Amendment states "the powers (County) not delegated to the United States by the Constitution, nor prohibited by it (Constitution) to the Counties (legislature), are reserved (reserved power clause) to the Counties (legislature) respectively, or to the County people (quasi equal populated districts)."

In other words, "the powers (County) not delegated to the United States by the Constitution, or not prohibited (not allowed) by it (Constitution) to the Counties (legislature), are reserved (reserved power clause) to the Counties (legislature) respectively, or to the County people (quasi equal populated districts)."

In other words, "the powers (County) not delegated to the United States by the Constitution, or not allowed by it (Constitution) to the Counties (legislature), are reserved (reserved power clause) to the Counties (legislature) respectively, or to the County people (quasi equal populated districts)."

In other words, "the powers (County) not delegated to the United States by the Constitution, or allowed by it (Constitution) to the Counties (legislature), are reserved

(reserved power clause) to the Counties (legislature) respectively, or to the County people (quasi equal populated districts)."

The "reserved power clause" applies to the County legislature (quasi equal populated districts) or to the County people (quasi equal populated districts).

The "reserved power clause" may be applied in the following two ways:

Rescind "right to life amendment" through the County legislature where the 60-40 voting prevails counting the number of voting legislature members

Rescind "right to life amendment" through the County people voting within "quasi equal populated districts" where the 60%-40% rule prevails of counting the number of winning "quasi equal populated districts" must be in forced to rescind a County "right to life amendment"

The "reserved power clause" is based upon the "power of representation" within "quasi equal populate districts." Any judgment against the County "rescind right to life amendment" violates the "power of representation" within the County people "quasi equal populated districts."

Constitution

Bill of Rights

10th Amendment

Delegated Clause (Constant)

Reserve Power Clause (City Rescind Right to Life Amendment)

RESERVE POWER CLAUSE
City Rescind Right to Life Amendment

(A City government has the power to rescind a "right to life" amendment.)

The 10th Amendment states "the powers (City) not delegated to the United States by the Constitution, nor prohibited by it (Constitution) to the Cities (council), are reserved (reserved power clause) to the Cities (council) respectively, or to the city people (quasi equal populated districts)."

In other words, "the powers (City) not delegated to the United States by the Constitution, or not prohibited (not allowed) by it (Constitution) to the Cities (council), are reserved (reserved power clause) to the Cities (council) respectively, or to the city people (quasi equal populated districts)."

In other words, "the powers (City) not delegated to the United States by the Constitution, or <u>not</u> allowed by it (Constitution) to the Cities (council), are reserved (reserved power clause) to the Cities (council) respectively, or to the city people (quasi equal populated districts)."

In other words, "the powers (City) not delegated to the United States by the Constitution, or allowed by it (Constitution) to the Cities (council), are reserved (reserved power clause) to the Cities (council) respectively, or to the city people (quasi equal populated districts)."

The "reserved power clause" applies to the city council (quasi equal populated districts) or to the city people (quasi equal populated districts).

The "reserved power clause" may be applied in the following two ways:

Rescind "right to life amendment" through the City council where the 60-40 voting prevails counting the number of voting council members

Rescind "right to life amendment" through the City people voting within "quasi equal populated districts" where the 60%-40% rule prevails of counting the number of winning "quasi equal populated districts" must be in forced to rescind a city "right to life amendment."

The "reserved power clause" is based upon the "power of representation" within "quasi equal populate districts." Any judgment against the City "rescind right to life amendment" violates the "power of representation" within the City people "quasi equal populated districts."

Constitution

Bill of Rights

10th Amendment

Delegated Clause (Constant)

Reserve Power Clause (Town Rescind Right to Life Amendment)

RESERVE POWER CLAUSE
Town Rescind Right to Life Amendment

(A Town government has the power to rescind a "right to life" amendment.)

The 10th Amendment states "the powers (Town) not delegated to the United States by the Constitution, nor prohibited by it (Constitution) to the Towns (council), are reserved (reserved power clause) to the Towns (council) respectively, or to the Town people (quasi equal populated districts)."

In other words, "the powers (Town) not delegated to the United States by the Constitution, or not prohibited (not allowed) by it (Constitution) to the Towns (council), are reserved (reserved power clause) to the Towns (council) respectively, or to the Town people (quasi equal populated districts)."

In other words, "the powers (Town) not delegated to the United States by the Constitution, or not allowed by it (Constitution) to the Towns (council), are reserved (reserved power clause) to the Towns (council) respectively, or to the Town people (quasi equal populated districts)."

In other words, "the powers (Town) not delegated to the United States by the Constitution, or allowed by it (Constitution) to the Towns (council), are reserved (reserved power clause) to the Towns (council) respectively, or to the Town people (quasi equal populated districts)."

The "reserved power clause" applies to the Town council (quasi equal populated districts) or to the Town people (quasi equal populated districts).

The "reserved power clause" may be applied in the following two ways:

Rescind "right to life amendment" through the Town council where the 60-40 voting prevails counting the number of voting council members

Rescind "right to life amendment" through the Town people voting within "quasi equal populated districts" where the 60%-40% rule prevails of counting the number of winning "quasi equal populated districts" must be in forced to rescind a Town amendment

The "reserved power clause" is based upon the "power of representation" within "quasi equal populate districts." Any judgment against the "Town rescind right to life amendment" violates the "power of representation" within the Town people "quasi equal populated districts."

Constitution

Bill of Rights

10th Amendment

Delegated Clause (Constant)

Reserve Power Clause (Village Rescind Right to Life Amendment)

RESERVE POWER CLAUSE
Village Rescind Right to Life Amendment

(A Village government has the power to rescind a "right to life" amendment.)

The 10th Amendment states "the powers (Village) not delegated to the United States by the Constitution, nor prohibited by it (Constitution) to the Villages (council), are reserved (reserved power clause) to the Villages (council) respectively, or to the Village people (quasi equal populated districts)."

In other words, "the powers (Village) not delegated to the United States by the Constitution, or not prohibited (not allowed) by it (Constitution) to the Villages (council), are reserved (reserved power clause) to the Villages (council) respectively, or to the Village people (quasi equal populated districts)."

In other words, "the powers (Village) not delegated to the United States by the Constitution, or not allowed by it (Constitution) to the Villages (council), are reserved (reserved power clause) to the Villages (council) respectively, or to the Village people (quasi equal populated districts)."

In other words, "the powers (Village) not delegated to the United States by the Constitution, or allowed by it (Constitution) to the Villages (council), are reserved (reserved

power clause) to the Villages (council) respectively, or to the Village people (quasi equal populated districts)."

The "reserved power clause" applies to the Village council (quasi equal populated districts) or to the Village people (quasi equal populated districts).

The "reserved power clause" may be applied in the following two ways:

Rescind "right to life amendment" through the Village council where the 60-40 voting prevails counting the number of voting council members

Rescind "right to life amendment" through the Village people voting within "quasi equal populated districts" where the 60%-40% rule prevails of counting the number of winning "quasi equal populated districts" must be in forced to rescind a Village amendment

The "reserved power clause" is based upon the "power of representation" within "quasi equal populate districts." Any judgment against the "Village rescind right to life amendment" violates the "power of representation" within the Village people "quasi equal populated districts."

"Reserved Power Clause"

Rescind Abortion Amendment

(State, County, City, Town, Village)

Constitution

Bill of Rights

10th Amendment

Delegated Clause (Constant)

Reserve Power Clause (State Rescind Abortion Amendment)

RESERVE POWER CLAUSE
State Rescind Abortion Amendment

(A State government has the power to rescind an abortion amendment.)

The 10th Amendment states "the powers (State) not delegated to the United States by the Constitution, nor prohibited by it (Constitution) to the States (legislature), are reserved (reserved power clause) to the States (legislature) respectively, or to the State people (quasi equal populated districts)."

In other words, "the powers (State) not delegated to the United States by the Constitution, or <u>not prohibited</u> (not allowed) by it (Constitution) to the States (legislature), are reserved (reserved power clause) to the States (legislature) respectively, or to the State people (quasi equal populated districts)."

In other words, "the powers (State) not delegated to the United States by the Constitution, or <u>not</u> allowed by it (Constitution) to the States (legislature), are reserved (reserved power clause) to the States (legislature) respectively, or to the State people (quasi equal populated districts)."

In other words, "the powers (State) not delegated to the United States by the Constitution, or allowed by it (Constitution) to the States (legislature), are reserved (reserved power clause) to the States (legislature) respectively, or to the State people (quasi equal populated districts)."

The "reserved power clause" applies to the State legislature (quasi equal populated districts) or to the State people (quasi equal populated districts).

The "reserved power clause" may be applied in the following two ways:

Rescind "abortion amendment" through the State legislature where the 60-40 voting prevails counting the number of voting legislature members

Rescind "abortion amendment" through the State people voting within "quasi equal populated districts" where the 60%-40% rule prevails of counting the number of winning "quasi equal populated districts" must be in forced to rescind a State "abortion amendment"

The "reserved power clause" is based upon the "power of representation" within "quasi equal populate districts." Any judgment against the "State rescind abortion amendment" violates the "power of representation" within the State people "quasi equal populated districts."

Constitution

Bill of Rights

10th Amendment

Delegated Clause (Constant)

Reserve Power Clause (County Rescind Abortion Amendment)

RESERVE POWER CLAUSE

County Rescind Abortion Amendment

(A County government has the power to rescind an abortion amendment.)

The 10th Amendment states "the powers (County) not delegated to the United States by the Constitution, nor prohibited by it (Constitution) to the Counties (legislature), are reserved (reserved power clause) to the Counties (legislature) respectively, or to the County people (quasi equal populated districts)."

In other words, "the powers (County) not delegated to the United States by the Constitution, or not prohibited (not allowed) by it (Constitution) to the Counties (legislature), are reserved (reserved power clause) to the Counties (legislature) respectively, or to the County people (quasi equal populated districts)."

In other words, "the powers (County) not delegated to the United States by the Constitution, or <u>not</u> allowed by it (Constitution) to the Counties (legislature), are reserved (reserved power clause) to the Counties (legislature) respectively, or to the County people (quasi equal populated districts)."

In other words, "the powers (County) not delegated to the United States by the Constitution, or allowed by it (Constitution) to the Counties (legislature), are reserved (reserved power clause) to the Counties (legislature) respectively, or to the County people (quasi equal populated districts)."

The "reserved power clause" applies to the County legislature (quasi equal populated districts) or to the County people (quasi equal populated districts).

The "reserved power clause" may be applied in the following two ways:

Rescind "abortion amendment" through the County legislature where the 60-40 voting prevails counting the number of voting legislature members

Rescind "abortion amendment" through the County people voting within "quasi equal populated districts" where the 60%-40% rule prevails of counting the number of winning "quasi equal populated districts" must be in forced to rescind a County "abortion amendment"

The "reserved power clause" is based upon the "power of representation" within "quasi equal populate districts." Any judgment against the "County rescind abortion amendment" violates the "power of representation" within the County people "quasi equal populated districts."

Constitution

Bill of Rights

10th Amendment

Delegated Clause (Constant)

Reserve Power Clause (City Rescind Abortion Amendment)

RESERVE POWER CLAUSE
City Rescind Abortion Amendment

(A City government has the power to rescind an abortion amendment.)

The 10th Amendment states "the powers (City) not delegated to the United States by the Constitution, nor prohibited by it (Constitution) to the Cities (council), are reserved (reserved power clause) to the Cities (council) respectively, or to the city people (quasi equal populated districts)."

In other words, "the powers (City) not delegated to the United States by the Constitution, or not prohibited (not allowed) by it (Constitution) to the Cities (council), are reserved (reserved power clause) to the Cities (council) respectively, or to the city people (quasi equal populated districts)."

In other words, "the powers (City) not delegated to the United States by the Constitution, or <u>not</u> allowed by it (Constitution) to

the Cities (council), are reserved (reserved power clause) to the Cities (council) respectively, or to the city people (quasi equal populated districts)."

In other words, "the powers (City) not delegated to the United States by the Constitution, or allowed by it (Constitution) to the Cities (council), are reserved (reserved power clause) to the Cities (council) respectively, or to the city people (quasi equal populated districts)." The "reserved power clause" applies to the city council (quasi equal populated districts) or to the city people (quasi equal populated districts).

The "reserved power clause" may be applied in the following two ways:

Rescind "abortion amendment" through the city council where the 60-40 voting prevails counting the number of voting council members

Rescind "abortion amendment" through the City people voting within "quasi equal populated districts" where the 60%-40% rule prevails of counting the number of winning "quasi equal populated districts" must be in forced to rescind a city amendment

The "reserved power clause" is based upon the "power of representation" within "quasi equal populate districts." Any judgment against the "City rescind abortion amendment" violates the "power of representation" within the city people "quasi equal populated districts."

Constitution

Bill of Rights

10th Amendment

Delegated Clause (Constant)

Reserve Power Clause (Town Rescind Abortion Amendment)

RESERVE POWER CLAUSE
Town Rescind Abortion Amendment

(A Town government has the power to rescind an abortion amendment.)

The 10th Amendment states "the powers (Town) not delegated to the United States by the Constitution, nor prohibited by it (Constitution) to the Towns (council), are reserved (reserved power clause) to the Towns (council) respectively, or to the Town people (quasi equal populated districts)."

In other words, "the powers (Town) not delegated to the United States by the Constitution, or not prohibited (not allowed) by it (Constitution) to the Towns (council), are reserved (reserved power clause) to the Towns (council) respectively, or to the Town people."

In other words, "the powers (Town) not delegated to the United States by the Constitution, or <u>not</u> allowed by it (Constitution) to the Towns (council), are reserved (reserved power clause) to the Towns (council) respectively, or to the Town people (quasi equal populated districts)."

In other words, "the powers (Town) not delegated to the United States by the Constitution, or allowed by it (Constitution) to the Towns (council), are reserved (reserved power clause) to the Towns (council) respectively, or to the Town people (quasi equal populated districts)."

The "reserved power clause" applies to the Town council (quasi equal populated districts) or to the Town people (quasi equal populated districts).

The "reserved power clause" may be applied in the following two ways:

Rescind "abortion amendment" through the Town council where the 60-40 voting prevails counting the number of voting council members

Rescind "abortion amendment" through the Town people voting within "quasi equal populated districts" where the 60%-40% rule prevails of counting the number of winning "quasi equal populated districts" must be in forced to rescind a Town amendment

The "reserved power clause" is based upon the "power of representation" within "quasi equal populate districts." Any

judgment against the "Town rescind abortion amendment" violates the "power of representation" within the Town people "quasi equal populated districts."

Constitution

Bill of Rights

10th Amendment

Delegated Clause (Constant)

Reserve Power Clause (Village Rescind Abortion Amendment)

RESERVE POWER CLAUSE
Village Rescind Abortion Amendment

(A Village government has the power to rescind an abortion amendment.)

The 10th Amendment states "the powers (Village) not delegated to the United States by the Constitution, nor prohibited by it (Constitution) to the Villages (council), are reserved (reserved power clause) to the Villages (council) respectively, or to the Village people (quasi equal populated districts)."

In other words, "the powers (Village) not delegated to the United States by the Constitution, or not prohibited (not allowed) by it (Constitution) to the Villages (council), are reserved (reserved power clause) to the Villages (council) respectively, or to the Village people (quasi equal populated districts)."

In other words, "the powers (Village) not delegated to the United States by the Constitution, or not allowed by it (Constitution) to the Villages (council), are reserved (reserved power clause) to the Villages (council) respectively, or to the Village people (quasi equal populated districts)."

In other words, "the powers (Village) not delegated to the United States by the Constitution, or allowed by it (Constitution) to the Villages (council), are reserved (reserved power clause) to the Villages (council) respectively, or to the Village people (quasi equal populated districts)."

The "reserved power clause" applies to the Village council (quasi equal populated districts) or to the Village people (quasi equal populated districts).

The "reserved power clause" may be applied in the following two ways:

Rescind "abortion amendment" through the Village council where the 60-40 voting prevails counting the number of voting council members

Rescind "abortion amendment" through the Village people voting within "quasi equal populated districts" where the 60%-40% rule prevails of counting the number of winning "quasi equal populated districts" must be in forced to rescind a Village amendment

The "reserved power clause" is based upon the "power of representation" within "quasi equal populate districts." Any

judgment against the "Village rescind abortion amendment" violates the "power of representation" within the Village people "quasi equal populated districts."

“Reserved Power Clause”

Repeal Right to Life Amendment

(State, County, City, Town, Village)

Constitution

Bill of Rights

10th Amendment

Delegated Clause (Constant)

Reserve Power Clause (State Repeal Right to Life Amendment)

RESERVE POWER CLAUSE
State Repeal Right to Life Amendment

(A State government has the power to repeal a "right to life" amendment.)

The 10th Amendment states "the powers (State) not delegated to the United States by the Constitution, nor prohibited by it (Constitution) to the States (legislature), are reserved (reserved power clause) to the States (legislature) respectively, or to the State people (quasi equal populated districts)."

In other words, "the powers (State) not delegated to the United States by the Constitution, or not prohibited (not allowed) by it (Constitution) to the States (legislature), are reserved (reserved power clause) to the States (legislature) respectively, or to the State people (quasi equal populated districts)."

In other words, "the powers (State) not delegated to the United States by the Constitution, or not allowed by it (Constitution) to the States (legislature), are reserved (reserved power clause) to the States (legislature) respectively, or to the State people (quasi equal populated districts)."

In other words, "the powers (State) not delegated to the United States by the Constitution, or allowed by it (Constitution) to the States (legislature), are reserved (reserved power clause) to the States (legislature) respectively, or to the State people (quasi equal populated districts)."

The "reserved power clause" applies to the State legislature (quasi equal populated districts) or to the State people (quasi equal populated districts).

The "reserved power clause" may be applied in the following two ways:

Repeal "right to life amendment" through the State legislature where the 60-40 voting prevails counting the number of voting legislature members

Repeal "right to life amendment" through the State people voting within "quasi equal populated districts" where the 60%-40% rule prevails of counting the number of winning "quasi equal populated districts" must be in forced to repeal a state amendment

The "reserved power clause" is based upon the "power of representation" within "quasi equal populate districts." Any

judgment against the "State repeal right to life amendment" violates the "power of representation" within the State people "quasi equal populated districts."

Constitution

Bill of Rights

10th Amendment

Delegated Clause (Constant)

Reserve Power Clause (County Repeal Right to Life Amendment)

RESERVE POWER CLAUSE
County Repeal Right to Life Amendment

(A County government has the power to repeal a "right to life" amendment.)

The 10th Amendment states "the powers (County) not delegated to the United States by the Constitution, nor prohibited by it (Constitution) to the Counties (legislature), are reserved (reserved power clause) to the Counties (legislature) respectively, or to the County people (quasi equal populated districts)."

In other words, "the powers (County) not delegated to the United States by the Constitution, or not prohibited (not allowed) by it (Constitution) to the Counties (legislature), are reserved (reserved power clause) to the Counties (legislature) respectively, or to the County people (quasi equal populated districts)."

In other words, "the powers (County) not delegated to the United States by the Constitution, or not allowed by it (Constitution) to the Counties (legislature), are reserved (reserved power clause) to the Counties (legislature) respectively, or to the County people (quasi equal populated districts)."

In other words, "the powers (County) not delegated to the United States by the Constitution, or allowed by it (Constitution) to the Counties (legislature), are reserved

(reserved power clause) to the Counties (legislature) respectively, or to the County people (quasi equal populated districts)."

The "reserved power clause" applies to the County legislature (quasi equal populated districts) or to the County people (quasi equal populated districts).

The "reserved power clause" may be applied in the following two ways:

Repeal "right to life amendment" through the County legislature where the 60-40 voting prevails counting the number of voting legislature members

Repeal "right to life amendment" through the County people voting within "quasi equal populated districts" where the 60%-40% rule prevails of counting the number of winning "quasi equal populated districts" must be in forced to repeal a county amendment

The "reserved power clause" is based upon the "power of representation" within "quasi equal populate districts." Any judgment against the "County repeal right to life amendment" violates the "power of representation" within the County people "quasi equal populated districts."

Constitution

Bill of Rights

10th Amendment

Delegated Clause (Constant)

Reserve Power Clause (City Repeal Right to Life Amendment)

RESERVE POWER CLAUSE
City Repeal Right to Life Amendment

(A City government has the power to repeal a "right to life" amendment.)

The 10th Amendment states "the powers (City) not delegated to the United States by the Constitution, nor prohibited by it (Constitution) to the Cities (council), are reserved (reserved power clause) to the Cities (council) respectively, or to the city people (quasi equal populated districts)."

In other words, "the powers (City) not delegated to the United States by the Constitution, or not prohibited (not allowed) by it (Constitution) to the Cities (council), are reserved (reserved power clause) to the Cities (council) respectively, or to the city people (quasi equal populated districts)."

In other words, "the powers (City) not delegated to the United States by the Constitution, or not allowed by it (Constitution) to the Cities (council), are reserved (reserved power clause) to the Cities (council) respectively, or to the city people (quasi equal populated districts)."

In other words, "the powers (City) not delegated to the United States by the Constitution, or allowed by it (Constitution) to the Cities (council), are reserved (reserved power clause) to the Cities (council) respectively, or to the city people (quasi equal populated districts)."

The "reserved power clause" applies to the city council (quasi equal populated districts) or to the city people (quasi equal populated districts).

The "reserved power clause" may be applied in the following two ways:

Repeal "right to life amendment" through the City council where the 60-40 voting prevails counting the number of voting council members

Repeal "right to life amendment" through the City people voting within "quasi equal populated districts" where the 60%-40% rule prevails of counting the number of winning "quasi equal populated districts" must be in forced to repeal a city amendment

The "reserved power clause" is based upon the "power of representation" within "quasi equal populate districts." Any

judgment against the "City repeal right to life amendment" violates the "power of representation" within the City people "quasi equal populated districts."

Constitution

Bill of Rights

10th Amendment

Delegated Clause (Constant)

Reserve Power Clause (Town Repeal Right to Life Amendment)

RESERVE POWER CLAUSE
Town Repeal Right to Life Amendment

(A Town government has the power to repeal a "right to life" amendment.)

The 10th Amendment states "the powers (Town) not delegated to the United States by the Constitution, nor prohibited by it (Constitution) to the Towns (council), are reserved (reserved power clause) to the Towns (council) respectively, or to the Town people (quasi equal populated districts)."

In other words, "the powers (Town) not delegated to the United States by the Constitution, or not prohibited (not allowed) by it (Constitution) to the Towns (council), are reserved (reserved power clause) to the Towns (council) respectively, or to the Town people (quasi equal populated districts)."

In other words, "the powers (Town) not delegated to the United States by the Constitution, or not allowed by it (Constitution) to the Towns (council), are reserved (reserved power clause) to the Towns (council) respectively, or to the Town people (quasi equal populated districts)."

In other words, "the powers (Town) not delegated to the United States by the Constitution, or allowed by it (Constitution) to the Towns (council), are reserved (reserved power clause) to the Towns (council) respectively, or to the Town people (quasi equal populated districts)."

The "reserved power clause" applies to the Town council (quasi equal populated districts) or to the Town people (quasi equal populated districts).

The "reserved power clause" may be applied in the following two ways:

Repeal "right to life amendment" through the Town council where the 60-40 voting prevails counting the number of voting council members

Repeal "right to life amendment" through the Town people voting within "quasi equal populated districts" where the 60%-40% rule prevails of counting the number of winning "quasi equal populated districts" must be in forced to repeal a Town amendment

The "reserved power clause" is based upon the "power of representation" within "quasi equal populate districts." Any

judgment against the "Town repeal right to life amendment" violates the "power of representation" within the Town people "quasi equal populated districts."

Constitution

Bill of Rights

10th Amendment

Delegated Clause (Constant)
Reserve Power Clause (Villager Repeal Right to Life Amendment)

RESERVE POWER CLAUSE
Village Repeal Right to Life Amendment

(A Village government has the power to repeal a "right to life" amendment.)

The 10th Amendment states "the powers (Village) not delegated to the United States by the Constitution, nor prohibited by it (Constitution) to the Villages (council), are reserved (reserved power clause) to the Villages (council) respectively, or to the Village people (quasi equal populated districts)."

In other words, "the powers (Village) not delegated to the United States by the Constitution, or not prohibited (not allowed) by it (Constitution) to the Villages (council), are reserved (reserved power clause) to the Villages (council) respectively, or to the Village people (quasi equal populated districts)."

In other words, "the powers (Village) not delegated to the United States by the Constitution, or not allowed by it (Constitution) to the Villages (council), are reserved (reserved power clause) to the Villages (council) respectively, or to the Village people (quasi equal populated districts)."

In other words, "the powers (Village) not delegated to the United States by the Constitution, or allowed by it (Constitution) to the Villages (council), are reserved (reserved

power clause) to the Villages (council) respectively, or to the Village people (quasi equal populated districts)."

The "reserved power clause" applies to the Village council (quasi equal populated districts) or to the Village people (quasi equal populated districts).

The "reserved power clause" may be applied in the following two ways:

Repeal "right to life amendment" through the Village council where the 60-40 voting prevails counting the number of voting council members

Repeal "right to life amendment" through the Village people voting within "quasi equal populated districts" where the 60%-40% rule prevails of counting the number of winning "quasi equal populated districts" must be in forced to repeal a Village amendment

The "reserved power clause" is based upon the "power of representation" within "quasi equal populate districts." Any judgment against the "Village repeal right to life amendment" violates the "power of representation" within the Village people "quasi equal populated districts."

"Reserved Power Clause"

Repeal Abortion Amendment

(State, County, City, Town, Village)

Constitution

Bill of Rights

10th Amendment

Delegated Clause (Constant)
Reserve Power Clause (State Repeal Abortion Amendment)

RESERVE POWER CLAUSE
State Repeal Abortion Amendment

(A State government has the power to repeal an abortion amendment.)

The 10th Amendment states "the powers (State) not delegated to the United States by the Constitution, nor prohibited by it (Constitution) to the States (legislature), are reserved (reserved power clause) to the States (legislature) respectively, or to the State people (quasi equal populated districts)."

In other words, "the powers (State) not delegated to the United States by the Constitution, or not prohibited (not allowed) by it (Constitution) to the States (legislature), are reserved (reserved power clause) to the States (legislature) respectively, or to the State people (quasi equal populated districts)."

In other words, "the powers (State) not delegated to the United States by the Constitution, or not allowed by it (Constitution) to

the States (legislature), are reserved (reserved power clause) to the States (legislature) respectively, or to the State people (quasi equal populated districts)."

In other words, "the powers (State) not delegated to the United States by the Constitution, or allowed by it (Constitution) to the States (legislature), are reserved (reserved power clause) to the States (legislature) respectively, or to the State people (quasi equal populated districts)."

The "reserved power clause" applies to the State legislature (quasi equal populated districts) or to the State people (quasi equal populated districts).

The "reserved power clause" may be applied in the following two ways:

Repeal "abortion amendment" through the State legislature where the 60-40 voting prevails counting the number of voting legislature members

Repeal "abortion amendment" through the State people voting within "quasi equal populated districts" where the 60%-40% rule prevails of counting the number of winning "quasi equal populated districts" must be in forced to repeal a State "abortion amendment"

The "reserved power clause" is based upon the "power of representation" within "quasi equal populate districts." Any judgment against the "State repeal abortion amendment" violates the "power of representation" within the State people "quasi equal populated districts."

Constitution

Bill of Rights

10th Amendment

Delegated Clause (Constant)

Reserve Power Clause (County Repeal Abortion Amendment)

RESERVE POWER CLAUSE
County Repeal Abortion Amendment

(A County government has the power to repeal an abortion amendment.)

The 10th Amendment states "the powers (County) not delegated to the United States by the Constitution, nor prohibited by it (Constitution) to the Counties (legislature), are reserved (reserved power clause) to the Counties (legislature) respectively, or to the County people (quasi equal populated districts)."

In other words, "the powers (County) not delegated to the United States by the Constitution, or not prohibited (not allowed) by it (Constitution) to the Counties (legislature), are reserved (reserved power clause) to the Counties (legislature) respectively, or to the County people (quasi equal populated districts)."

In other words, "the powers (County) not delegated to the United States by the Constitution, or <u>not</u> allowed by it (Constitution) to the Counties (legislature), are reserved (reserved power clause) to the Counties (legislature) respectively, or to the County people (quasi equal populated districts)."

In other words, "the powers (County) not delegated to the United States by the Constitution, or allowed by it (Constitution) to the Counties (legislature), are reserved (reserved power clause) to the Counties (legislature)

respectively, or to the County people (quasi equal populated districts)."

The "reserved power clause" applies to the County legislature (quasi equal populated districts) or to the County people (quasi equal populated districts).

The "reserved power clause" may be applied in the following two ways:

Repeal "abortion amendment" through the County legislature where the 60-40 voting prevails counting the number of voting legislature members

Repeal "abortion amendment" through the County people voting within "quasi equal populated districts" where the 60%-40% rule prevails of counting the number of winning "quasi equal populated districts" must be in forced to repeal a County "abortion amendment"

The "reserved power clause" is based upon the "power of representation" within "quasi equal populate districts." Any judgment against the "County repeal abortion amendment" violates the "power of representation" within the County people "quasi equal populated districts."

Constitution

Bill of Rights

10th Amendment

Delegated Clause (Constant)

Reserve Power Clause (City Repeal Abortion Amendment)

RESERVE POWER CLAUSE
City Repeal Abortion Amendment

(A City government has the power to repeal an abortion amendment.)

The 10th Amendment states "the powers (City) not delegated to the United States by the Constitution, nor prohibited by it (Constitution) to the Cities (council), are reserved (reserved power clause) to the Cities (council) respectively, or to the city people (quasi equal populated districts)."

In other words, "the powers (City) not delegated to the United States by the Constitution, or not prohibited (not allowed) by it (Constitution) to the Cities (council), are reserved (reserved power clause) to the Cities (council) respectively, or to the city people (quasi equal populated districts)."

In other words, "the powers (City) not delegated to the United States by the Constitution, or <u>not</u> allowed by it (Constitution) to

the Cities (council), are reserved (reserved power clause) to the Cities (council) respectively, or to the city people (quasi equal populated districts)."

In other words, "the powers (City) not delegated to the United States by the Constitution, or allowed by it (Constitution) to the Cities (council), are reserved (reserved power clause) to the Cities (council) respectively, or to the city people (quasi equal populated districts)." The "reserved power clause" applies to the city council (quasi equal populated districts) or to the city people (quasi equal populated districts).

The "reserved power clause" may be applied in the following two ways:

Repeal "abortion amendment" through the city council where the 60-40 voting prevails counting the number of voting council members

Repeal "abortion amendment" through the City people voting within "quasi equal populated districts" where the 60%-40% rule prevails of counting the number of winning "quasi equal populated districts" must be in forced to repeal a city amendment

The "reserved power clause" is based upon the "power of representation" within "quasi equal populate districts." Any judgment against the "City repeal abortion amendment" violates the "power of representation" within the city people "quasi equal populated districts."

Constitution

Bill of Rights

10th Amendment

Delegated Clause (Constant)

Reserve Power Clause (Town Repeal Abortion Amendment)

RESERVE POWER CLAUSE
Town Repeal Abortion Amendment

(A Town government has the power to repeal an abortion amendment.)

The 10th Amendment states "the powers (Town) not delegated to the United States by the Constitution, nor prohibited by it (Constitution) to the Towns (council), are reserved (reserved power clause) to the Towns (council) respectively, or to the Town people (quasi equal populated districts)."

In other words, "the powers (Town) not delegated to the United States by the Constitution, or not prohibited (not allowed) by it (Constitution) to the Towns (council), are reserved (reserved power clause) to the Towns (council) respectively, or to the Town people (quasi equal populated districts)."

In other words, "the powers (Town) not delegated to the United States by the Constitution, or <u>not</u> allowed by it (Constitution) to the Towns (council), are reserved (reserved power clause) to the Towns (council) respectively, or to the Town people (quasi equal populated districts)."

In other words, "the powers (Town) not delegated to the United States by the Constitution, or allowed by it (Constitution) to the Towns (council), are reserved (reserved power clause) to the Towns (council) respectively, or to the Town people (quasi equal populated districts)." The "reserved power clause" applies to the Town council (quasi equal populated districts) or to the Town people (quasi equal populated districts).

The "reserved power clause" may be applied in the following two ways:

Repeal "abortion amendment" through the Town council where the 60-40 voting prevails counting the number of voting council members

Repeal "abortion amendment" through the Town people voting within "quasi equal populated districts" where the 60%-40% rule prevails of counting the number of winning "quasi equal populated districts" must be in forced to repeal a Town amendment

The "reserved power clause" is based upon the "power of representation" within "quasi equal populate districts." Any judgment against the "Town repeal abortion amendment" violates the "power of representation" within the Town people "quasi equal populated districts."

Constitution

Bill of Rights

10th Amendment

Delegated Clause (Constant)

Reserve Power Clause (Village Repeal Abortion Amendment)

RESERVE POWER CLAUSE
Village Repeal Abortion Amendment

(A Village government has the power to repeal an abortion amendment.)

The 10th Amendment states "the powers (Village) not delegated to the United States by the Constitution, nor prohibited by it (Constitution) to the Villages (council), are reserved (reserved power clause) to the Villages (council) respectively, or to the Village people (quasi equal populated districts)."

In other words, "the powers (Village) not delegated to the United States by the Constitution, or not prohibited (not allowed) by it (Constitution) to the Villages (council), are reserved (reserved power clause) to the Villages (council) respectively, or to the Village people (quasi equal populated districts)."

In other words, "the powers (Village) not delegated to the United States by the Constitution, or not allowed by it (Constitution) to the Villages (council), are reserved (reserved power clause) to the Villages (council) respectively, or to the Village people (quasi equal populated districts)."

In other words, "the powers (Village) not delegated to the United States by the Constitution, or allowed by it (Constitution) to the Villages (council), are reserved (reserved power clause) to the Villages (council) respectively, or to the Village people (quasi equal populated districts)."

The "reserved power clause" applies to the Village council (quasi equal populated districts) or to the Village people (quasi equal populated districts).

The "reserved power clause" may be applied in the following two ways:

Repeal "abortion amendment" through the Village council where the 60-40 voting prevails counting the number of voting council members

Repeal "abortion amendment" through the Village people voting within "quasi equal populated districts" where the 60%-40% rule prevails of counting the number of winning "quasi equal populated districts" must be in forced to repeal a Village amendment

The "reserved power clause" is based upon the "power of representation" within "quasi equal populate districts." Any

judgment against the "Village repeal abortion amendment" violates the "power of representation" within the Village people "quasi equal populated districts."

Constitution

Bill of Rights

10th Amendment

Delegated Clause (Constant)
Reserve Power Clause Variable
(State, County, City, Village)

The Constitution is a living breathing document through the "Reserved Power Clause" covering State, County, City, Village legislation!

Constitution

Bill of Rights

10th Amendment

Delegated Clause (Constant)

Article V Congressional Legislation

The Constitution is a living, breathing document through "Article V" covering congressional legislation.

THINK
POWER OF
REPRESENTATION

THINK
LIBERTY!

THINK REPUBLIC!

REFERENCES

- *17th Amendment… Rescind!!!* — Daniel H. Marchi
- *Past Future Power Belongs to the Reserved Power Clause* — Daniel H. Marchi
- *10th Amendment Secures a Republic Form of Government!!!* — Author, Daniel H. Marchi
- *This Book Places an Indictment on the Federal Government and 16th Amendment!!!* — Author, Daniel H. Marchi

www.ingramcontent.com/pod-product-compliance
Lightning Source LLC
LaVergne TN
LVHW051926051126
851857LV00020B/2039
* 9 7 9 8 8 9 6 7 2 3 0 4 2 *